Ben Sharples is a Partner in Michelmores' Agriculture team and heads the Firm's Natural Capital Group. He is dual-qualified having originally trained as a Chartered Surveyor and Valuer before becoming a Solicitor. Ben brings legal, estate management, environmental and valuation expertise to the issue of structuring deals. Ben has spent over 25 years advising clients on their use of the oldest asset, land, and is now assisting them with the emergence of the latest asset class in the form of natural capital.

Ben is recognised as a leading advisor in this emerging cross-sector discipline and he sits on both the Property and Environment & Land Use Committees of the Central Association of Agricultural Valuers. Ben was one of the first lawyers to engage with emergent policy on natural capital and has been the architect in several novel natural capital schemes that have now become the norm.

A Practical Guide to Payments for Environmental Services

A Practical Guide to Payments for Environmental Services

Ben Sharples FRICS FAAV FCIArb

Solicitor Advocate

(Higher Court Civil Proceedings)

Law Brief Publishing

Published 2024 by Law Brief Publishing, an imprint of Law Brief Publishing Ltd
30 The Parks
Minehead
Somerset
TA24 8BT

www.lawbriefpublishing.com

Paperback: 978-1-916698-00-0

To my family. This is only a small book, but I know you have made big sacrifices. Thank you.

PREFACE

This book is intended to be a helpful companion to practitioners advising clients on the many and varied opportunities that exist in the market for environmental services. The question that I am asked most regularly is "how do we monetise these opportunities?" I doubt that I am the only adviser being asked this.

The issue of commercial advice is the responsibility of surveyors and consultants so this book is not about deal making but it aims to assist with the understanding of such deals. The lawyer's job remains that of sensibly drafting and structuring arrangements so that the practical benefits of environmental improvement can be delivered hand in glove with financial return.

I have tried to look at the various issues from the perspective of those who own, rent and occupy land for it is they who control the original and oldest asset from which has emerged the newest class of natural capital. As the saying goes, they are not making land anymore, but new ways are being found to utilise it.

Participants in these new markets will have to learn how to combine the streams of public and private money to best advantage and to navigate the rules many of which are yet to be drafted.

The role of tenants in meeting the challenges of climate change and loss of biodiversity is vital and I have stressed within the following pages and elsewhere that collaboration is key in the absence of agricultural legislation which has not kept pace with the last century never mind the current one.

Existing markets will be considered but the structuring advice must try and anticipate how the market for environmental services may evolve so that future opportunities can be exploited and the rewards apportioned appropriately.

The agricultural sector has a huge role to play in meeting the challenges that lie ahead and the opportunities are just as sizable. I hope this book is of some help to those helping their clients create a more sustainable rural economy. Perhaps it might also assist a group of individuals with whom I have always sympathised – those taking on exams for academic or professional qualifications.

I am indebted to Gilliam Collinsworth-Hamilton who has provided invaluable help with research and gathering information as well as being a great sounding board and editor. My partners, Cathy Bryant and Iwan Williams have provided insight on taxation matters and as ever, when it comes to this book, the credit is theirs and the mistakes are mine.

One of the aspects of working in this sector is the breadth of expertise needed to properly advise clients. Having previously only swum in the rather small pond of agricultural litigation I am now working with a much larger circle of colleagues both internally and at other firms.

Leading the Natural Capital Team at Michelmores has reinforced what great colleagues I work with. In particular, I must thank my partners on the commercial side of the business Ian Holyoak, Alex Watson and Chloe Vernon-Shore ably assisted by Katharine Everett-Nunns, Ed Wilson and Harriet Grimes. I have worked with Adam Corbin, Viv Williams, Josie Edwards and Rachel O'Connor for longer than they care to remember and I am very grateful to them and the rest of the Agriculture Team for their support.

I have attempted to state the law as at 6 June 2024.

Ben Sharples
June 2024

CONTENTS

CHAPTER ONE

REVIEW OF CURRENT LANDSCAPE

While development of both urban and rural landscapes have contributed to climate change and biodiversity loss, it is in the rural environment that one finds the potential to unlock large scale mitigation solutions. Such solutions can be found through payments for environmental services arising from changing land management practices.

Environmental services and their associated revenues involve the utilisation of natural capital assets which are, in the main, managed and controlled by landowners and farmers. To understand this nascent marketplace, it is therefore necessary to consider natural capital and how its utilisation can fit in with the rapidly changing agricultural sector, as well as how the sector receives governmental support. The Government's policy shift from production-based incentives to "*public money for public goods*[1]" in particular is worth closer scrutiny.

More broadly, the UK's exit from the EU has given the Government greater flexibility in implementation of domestic agricultural policies. This provides the UK with the opportunity to not only reshape its agricultural and environmental policies through devolved powers but also to pick a new pathway through the maze of European legislation and caselaw.

This time of seismic change provides a great opportunity for those tasked with the management of rural land. The preference of government seems to be that the private sector lead the way in how the markets for nature-

---

1 Agriculture Bill to boost environment and food production – GOV.UK (www.gov.uk)

based solutions develop so there is a certain requirement to run with the ball and frankly, get on with it.

What is Natural Capital?

Natural capital represents "the stock of renewable and non-renewable natural resources that combine to yield a flow of ecosystem services."[2] It can be more easily explained by breaking down the term into its individual components. "Natural" in this context refers to the natural world and its resources, in contrast to man-made. "Capital" is a store of wealth which can also be used to generate value. A computer holds value not just because of its physical components, but also because it can be used to create other valuable assets. A woodland is valuable not just for its timber, but also because of its myriad environmental benefits, from enriching local biodiversity to combating climate change by capturing carbon. A computer is capital; a woodland is natural capital.

Unfortunately, while natural capital may produce benefits which are critically important to the wellbeing of the planet, these benefits may come at a financial opportunity cost to the owner. Preventing livestock from grazing near a riverbed may be good for the river, but it limits the grazing land available to the farmer and therefore the revenue which can be generated from the land. While we are all conscious of the long-term costs of environmental degradation, we must also pay our bills. Furthermore, the burden of transitioning to a more environmentally sustainable national economy is not borne equally by all economic participants: it's one thing to ask urban residents to be more judicious in sorting their rubbish, and another to ask a farmer to leave acres of their land ungrazed for the greater good.

In recent years, governments have sought to better align these economic and environmental incentives by introducing schemes that allow

---

2 McGrath, L. and Hynes, S. 2020. "Approaches to accounting for our natural capital: Applications across Ireland." Biology and Environment: Proceedings of the Royal Irish Academy 2020.

landowners to monetize their natural capital. Tax write-offs help offset losses incurred by foregoing development, while nascent biodiversity and carbon marketplaces provide income to landowners via the biodiversity units and carbon credits generated by more environmentally friendly uses of their land. By recognizing and commodifying the value of natural capital, governments are making it easier for landowners to make environmentally friendly decisions without sacrificing their own livelihoods.

The Agricultural Sector

There is a long history of political influence in the agricultural sector. The Corn Laws, passed in 1815, attempted to alleviate the strains placed on the industry by the Napoleonic Wars. The laws included government-imposed tariffs on imported grain, which artificially propped up the domestic market. The Corn Laws were repealed in 1846, largely due to the Irish Famine. Surprisingly, there was no resulting plunge in domestic grain prices, underscoring how markets don't always behave as expected; this was an early lesson in the difficulties of controlling the price of basic commodities.

While this book is will not go through the evolution of UK agricultural policy in detail, it is helpful to identify the main historical links in the chain of events leading to the present day. Suffice it to say attention was focused on maximising production even before Britain joined the European Economic Community ("**EEC**") in 1973.

These main links in the chain are:

- Second World War
- EEC Membership 1973
- MacSharry Reforms – 1991
- Agenda 2000 – 1999

- Mid Term Review – 2003
- Single Payment Scheme – 2005
- CAP Health Check – 2009
- Basic Payment Scheme – 2015
- Brexit – 31 January 2020
- Agriculture Act 2020
- Transition Period 2021-2028

UK Environmental Land Management Schemes (ELMS)

A brief history of UK agricultural policy

The modern framework for governmental influence over national agriculture markets was born from the experiences of the Second World War, where the UK in particular experienced significant food shortages. These experiences shaped the Agricultural Holdings Act 1948, with its focus on production and the rules of good husbandry.

The policy focus on production continued throughout the 1950's and 60's. Farmers were offered grants for removing hedgerows and ploughing up grassland with a higher rate of £30 per hectare.[3] It is fair to say that carbon sequestration was not high on the agenda at the time. Some did call[4] for preservation of grassland, but only in the context of its ability to support a greater national beef herd and sheep flock.

3 Agriculture (Ploughing Grants) Act 1952

4 AGRICULTURE (PLOUGHING GRANTS) (Hansard, 21 October 1952) (parliament.uk)

A significant development was UK membership of the EEC in 1973. All members—including the UK—were subject to the Common Agricultural Policy ("**CAP**"), a negotiated policy which sought to balance trade between member countries whilst keeping their individual agricultural sectors afloat through export subsidies and other price support.

This interventionist method of propping up commodity prices eventually became the subject of considerable criticism. References to "*wine lakes*" and "*butter mountains*" were commonplace, as EU member states had the ability to place agricultural commodities, such as beef and dairy products, into storage. This had the effect of artificially supporting the price by reducing supply. The theory was that the stocks could be released onto the market when prices recovered; however, in practice, the mere knowledge that such supply exists applied downward pressure to market prices, as buyers knew the market could be flooded with supply if prices increased too rapidly. Whilst the EU Commission has since tried to reduce reliance on intervention buying, it is worth noting that the UK Government has specifically reserved a power to intervene in the market in the Agriculture Act 2020[5].

Mounting stocks of agricultural commodities led to the MacSharry Reforms in 1992, in which then-Agriculture Commissioner Ray MacSharry published a paper[6] setting out wide-ranging problems with the system. Many of these issues were caused by government subsidies that were tied to production, driving supply beyond demand levels and leading to gluts in the market. Production-linked subsidies also encouraged economies of scale, prompting industry consolidation and driving out smaller businesses.

The MacSharry Reforms included cuts to support prices (which were replaced by direct payments to farmers) and the introduction of set-aside,

5 Section 21 (3) Agriculture Act 2020

6 The Development and Future of the CAP

where producers would only qualify for such payments if they took a percentage of their land out of arable production. Schemes were introduced across a wide range of agricultural products, ranging from sheep and beef to arable crops.

The set aside rate—the percentage of land that must be set aside for farms to qualify for the subsidy—was originally set at 15%, then reduced to 10% in 1996. In 2000, the EU set about making major reforms to the CAP under what it called "Agenda 2000;" however the set-aside rate remained unchanged until the Mid Term Review in 2005, where it was reduced to 8%. It was finally reduced to 0% in 2008 before being abolished later that year as part of the CAP Health Check.

While Agenda 2000 left the set-aside rate unchecked, it did take a hatchet to support prices for commodities and diverted those funds to direct payments to farmers. The CAP budget was also split into two "pillars" of production support and rural development. It is the second pillar which funded the rural development programme and environmental schemes under CAP.

Since the implementation of the Mid Term Review in 2005, most of the direct payment schemes were amalgamated into an area-based scheme, the Single Payment Scheme, which was renamed the Basic Payment Scheme in 2015. In England, this resulted in a swift move away from production-based subsidies. Wales and Scotland took a more gradual route to an area-based scheme, likely due to their increased need to support upland farms.

The CAP has been subject to major and seemingly continual reforms in recent years. The most significant change has been the shift from support of the commodity to support of the producer, with the quantum leap in this regard being the introduction of the Single Farm Payment under the Mid-term Review of the Common Agricultural Policy[7]. A key

7 European Commission Mid-term Review of the Common Agricultural Policy COM(2002)394

characteristic of the Single Farm Payment was that it could be claimed by producers, even though they were not producing any commodities at all. There was a requirement that a claimant be a farmer and one who was exercising an "agricultural activity." However, simply keeping the land in "good agricultural and environmental condition" constituted such an activity, so there was no imperative to actually grow a crop.

This evolution continued, with the Basic Payment Scheme also being decoupled from production, but the Agriculture Act has taken it a step further with the direct payments being decoupled from the occupation of land itself.[8]

Agricultural policy post-Brexit

Until this point, the UK's agricultural policy was unable to deviate from that of the EU. This changed following the UK's exit from the EU on 31 January 2020.

There was much discussion as to the shape of future agricultural support during the period between the vote to leave the EU and the UK's actual departure. Policymakers eventually decided that the UK would move from area and production-based support to the policy of "public money for public goods", with a strong emphasis on protection of the environment. Such a major change in direction would potentially have quite a severe impact on producers, so the Government elected to introduce the new system over a seven-year agricultural transition period from 2021-2028. This transition involved gradual changes to the existing Basic Payment Scheme, the simultaneous running of pilots of the new ELMS scheme and an eventual transfer between the two by 2028.

---

8 Section 12 of the Agriculture Act 2020

The UK Transition Period until 31 December 2020

The UK's departure from the EU is on the terms of the Withdrawal Agreement,[9] which provides for a transitional period lasting until 31 December 2020.

During that period, the UK Government confirmed[10] that the Basic Payment Scheme (BPS) will remain largely unaltered, having provided a funding guarantee. This safety net was critical as, under the terms of the Withdrawal Agreement, all EU funding for direct payments (formerly CAP Pillar 1 payments) in 2020 would move to be under domestic control one year before all other EU policy areas, as CAP expenditure was paid for out of the following year's EU budget. EU CAP subsidies were divided into those paid under Pillar 1 (direct schemes) and Pillar 2 (rural development schemes).

Since then, we have seen the enactment of the Agriculture Act 2020 and the Environment Act 2021 together with relevant secondary legislation. This legislation is shaping the new landscape in which farmers and landowners are now operating and they are having to learn to comply with a different set of rules and regulations.

Mixing and Matching Credits: Stacking, Bundling and Additionality

The use of public money to procure services from farmers and landowners has the potential to be a controversial topic and it is certain that any payments for environmental services will be closely scrutinised. The slightest suggestion of greenwashing or double counting will be equally unwelcome to civil servants or their counterparts in private commerce. There has already been much discussion of the additionality principle which in simple terms means a landowner will only be rewarded

---

9 *Agreement on the withdrawal of the United Kingdom of Great Britain and Northern Ireland from the European Union and the European Atomic Energy Community*, which was signed on 24 January 2020.

10 Clause 12 of the 2019 Agriculture Bill

for benefits accruing from a new and quantifiable environmental input. There will be no reward for habitat or trees that would have been in existence anyway.

As such, a number of principles have been identified in order to ensure such market integrity and the key one is additionality.

This is a phrase which is often encountered and it is probably worth taking some time to properly understand the issues. Additionality, could, simplistically be viewed as ensuring that Mother Nature gets her money's worth. That is, money invested in natural capital inputs must lead directly to environmental improvement.

There are various additionality tests which have arisen through the operation of market schemes or from the various consultations that have taken place.

For example, the Woodland Carbon Code assesses additionality with a legal and investment test. Any new planting must not be required by way of an existing legal obligation and must be uneconomic without the carbon credit income.

Referenced in the BNG Consultation,[11] the Treasury Green Book[12] defines additionality as:

> *"a real increase in social value that would not have occurred in the absence of the intervention being appraised"*

The British Standard on BNG is more restrictive in that the Green Book would encompass benefits outside the ambit of BNG whereas here the definition is:

---

10 Consultation on Biodiversity Net Gain Regulations and Implementation_January2022.pdf (defra.gov.uk)

12 The Green Book (publishing.service.gov.uk)

> *"Property of measures to achieve biodiversity net gain, where the conservation outcomes it delivers are demonstrably new and additional and would not have resulted without it."*

The BNG Consultation is clear that any nature-based interventions which are already required by law or agreement cannot be used to support claims for BNG or other emerging markets.

Using an example to illustrate these points, if a landowner of Whiteacre has been required to plant trees to replace others felled due to development those trees cannot be used to claim carbon credits because they were required to be there as a result of a planning obligation. There is no additional benefit in the form of increased carbon sequestration hence no carbon credits.

Under the Green Book definition, a different landowner of Blackacre might take land out of agricultural production and claim nutrient neutrality credits as a result. The recent Government response and summary of responses to the BNG Consultation has indicated that BNG and nutrient neutrality credits may be sold from the same nature-based intervention. This means that if habitat is created on the former agricultural land then both those types of credits can be generated and sold. However, a landowner would not be able to claim soil carbon credits on the same area of land unless the carbon sequestration achieved would have happened in the absence of the nutrient neutrality and BNG measures set out above.

However, the same landowner could then plant trees on Blackacre (already being utilised for BNG and nutrient neutrality credits) and claim carbon credits as long as the trees are not required to contribute to the metric calculation for BNG purposes or are factored into the nutrient neutrality calculation as increasing phosphate or nitrogen uptake. If those criteria are satisfied then the trees are a new and additional nature based intervention and so the additionality rules are satisfied.

It should be noted that where Natural England insist on tree planting as part of a nutrient neutrality scheme then those trees could not be used for carbon credit purposes because they would have been there anyway as a result of the nutrient mitigation works.

Such principles then need to be implemented which requires rules, standards and governance.

The rules bring together the three most important factors for nature markets to succeed:

- Stacking and bundling;
- Additionality; and
- Blending of public and private finance.

Stacking

Stacking is where different types of credits are derived from one or more activities on the same piece of land. Using the example above, you could stack BNG, nutrient neutrality and carbon credits on Blackacre but the activities are different. The land is the constant on which the credits are stacked and there is no requirement that they emanate from the same nature-based intervention. Land managers will still need to navigate the stacking rules of individual schemes.

Bundling

Bundling is where several different environmental benefits are combined in a single credit. The bundle may be explicit in that the separate benefits are identified and quantified or it may be implicit in that only one benefit is identified with everything else thrown in as part of the deal.

An example of an implicit bundle is the offering under the UK Woodland Carbon Code where the wider benefits of woodland creation are sold along with the carbon. It seems doubtful that such generous terms will continue much longer.

The Nature Markets Framework[13] issued by the Government commits to greater use of stacking and explicit bundling as it encourages efficient land use and environmental improvement. The additionality risks inherent in stacking and bundling are identified in that subsequent habitat improvement must be delivered on top of an initial activity – as I set out above in the Blackacre example. As that shows, the greatest jeopardy lies in the mixing of regulatory and voluntary markets and this aspect will be kept under review.

Additionality

I have set out the existing additionality rules above and the Framework states that a move might be made to a single financial additionality test which could be applied across multiple nature markets. It appears that the concept of regulatory 2+2=5 which allows BNG and nutrient neutrality to be claimed from the same intervention will remain.

A single environmental project can advance multiple objectives simultaneously. Planting woodland, for example, both captures carbon and improves local biodiversity. Can its owner therefore use the same woodland to claim both BNG credits and carbon credits?

The principle of additionality requires that the benefits made by the improvement on which the landowner is relying to apply for a credit scheme would not have occurred in absence of the application. If the landowner planted woodland in order to meet another contractual or statutory obligation (e.g. to meet a "favourable condition" standard on land designated by Natural England as a "site of special scientific interest" (SSSI)),[14] the woodland would have improved local biodiversity

13 Nature markets: (publishing.service.gov.uk)

14 https://www.gov.uk/guidance/protected-areas-sites-of-special-scientific-interest

regardless of whether the landowner sought BNG credits and therefore would not qualify for the BNG scheme.

Different projects on the same site

It should be noted that the principle of additionality is project-specific, not site-specific. That is to say, if a landowner plants a woodland for carbon credits, they may then further improve the woodland from a habitat perspective to acquire BNG credits. Each improvement satisfies the additionality principle: carbon was captured in pursuit of carbon credits, and the site was further improved in pursuit of BNG credits; neither of these benefits would have occurred otherwise.

The government has provided guidance on combining different environmental payments;[15] however, as nature markets are in the early stages of development, this guidance is subject to change.

Stacking on protected habitats

Landowners may enhance land on which development is restricted (e.g. "Sustainable Alternative Natural Greenspaces" (SANG)[16] or SSSIs) to qualify for credits so long as the additionality principle is respected (a specific improvement is made to enhance the site) **provided the improvement does not disrupt existing protections.** [17]

---

15 https://www.gov.uk/guidance/combining-environmental-payments-biodiversity-net-gain-bng-and-nutrient-mitigation

16 https://www.woking2027.info/supplementary/tbhspaspd/updated_sang_guidance_August_2021.pdf

17 https://www.local.gov.uk/pas/topics/environment/biodiversity-net-gain-local-authorities/biodiversity-net-gain-faqs#additionality-stacking-and-natural-capital

Summary

- Landowners cannot claim multiple types of credits from the same improvement on the same piece of land.
- Landowners can claim multiple types of credits from different improvements on the same piece of land.
- Each activity must satisfy the principle of additionality to qualify for a distinct type of credit.
- New activities may not disrupt the benefits derived from existing improvements.

Natural capital markets are a nascent and growing field, many of these rules are based on government guidance and remain untested in law. Expect these rules to be modified and refined by precedent and additional legislation.

CHAPTER TWO

CARBON

<u>Overview</u>

- Human industrial activity produces large quantities of gasses as a byproduct which are released into the atmosphere. The cumulative effect of these gasses has been to alter the composition of our atmosphere, trapping heat in what is called the "greenhouse effect," contributing to dramatic changes within the Earth's climate.[18]

- To tackle this issue, the UK government has committed to fully offsetting greenhouse gas (GHG) emissions with projects to remove these gasses from the atmosphere by 2050, dubbed the UK's "net zero strategy."[19]

- Carbon dioxide (CO2) emissions are by far the largest contributor, accounting for 85% of all GHG emissions in the UK in 2021.[20] Tackling carbon emissions is therefore an essential component of the government's net zero strategy.

- However, many of the activities that emit the most carbon are also essential to keeping a country's economy afloat. Governments must therefore balance disincentivising carbon emissions with minimizing the risk of economic downturn.

---

18 https://www.britannica.com/science/greenhouse-gas

19 https://www.gov.uk/government/publications/net-zero-strategy/1-why-net-zero

https://www.ons.gov.uk/economy/environmentalaccounts/bulletins/greenhousegasintensityprovisionalestimatesuk/2021

Carbon credit markets are one possible solution: companies that reduce emissions and remove carbon from the atmosphere earn credits, which they can sell at market rate to companies that produce carbon.

- There are two distinct types of credit markets in the UK: the government-regulated emissions trading scheme (ETS) and unregulated voluntary carbon markets (VCMs)

Emissions Trading Scheme

Legal Framework[21]

- The Greenhouse Gas Emissions Trading Scheme Order 2020 (www.legislation.gov.uk/uksi/2020/1265/contents/made)

- The Greenhouse Gas Emissions Trading Scheme Auctioning Regulations 2021 (www.legislation.gov.uk/uksi/2021/484/contents/made)

Firms that carry out activities covered by the ETS must hold an emissions permit. Permits are divided into three categories: emissions, small emissions, and ultra-small emissions, each with different requirements. Which regulator oversees a firm's compliance depends on the firm's business activity and geographical location. Participants must then submit emissions reports which are verified by an accredited verifier. Non-compliance with ETS requirements may result in a civil penalty to be determined by the individual regulator.

[21] https://www.gov.uk/government/publications/participating-in-the-uk-ets/participating-in-the-uk-ets

Emitters

- **Eligibility.** The government divides participants into two categories: installations and aviation.

    - **Installations:**[22] This category applies to any stationary units in which the activities listed in schedule 2 of the Greenhouse Gas Emissions Trading Scheme Order are carried out. These activities range from aluminium production to thermal power production with an output exceeding 20MW;

    - **Aviation:**[23] This category applies to aircraft operators operating within the UK that exceed certain thresholds. These thresholds are different for commercial and non-commercial operators. Commercial operators that either operate fewer than 243 full-scope flights in a 4-month period for 3 consecutive periods or emit less than 10,000 tonnes of CO2 annually are exempt, as are non-commercial air transport operators with annual emissions of less than 1,000 tonnes are exempt. Certain specific flights (e.g. military) are also exempt.

- **System.** Regulators will issue firms with an allotment of free allowance credits; this allotment of "free credits" is meant to decrease each year. Further credits must be purchased at auction or on the secondary market. Participants hold accounts with the UK Emissions Trading Registry, which acts as a central ledger for credits. The registry contains both domestic allowance credits

---

22 https://www.gov.uk/government/publications/uk-emissions-trading-scheme-for-installations-how-to-comply

23 https://www.gov.uk/guidance/uk-emissions-trading-scheme-for-aviation-how-to-comply

and international units registered with the UK Kyoto Protocol Registry.

Small emitters[24]

- **Eligibility.** An installation may qualify as a small emitter if it emits less than 25,000 tonnes of carbon dioxide equivalent annually or has a total rated thermal input of less than 35MW (if applicable). An application must be approved by both the firm's regulator and the ETS authority. Aircraft operators cannot apply for small emitter status.
    - **Hospital providers:** An installation may qualify for a small emissions permit if at least 85% of the heat it produces is used by or supplied to one or more hospitals.
- **Benefits.** Small emitters are only subject to emissions targets and do not need to participate in the allowance credit scheme. If a small emitter reports emissions below their annual target, any credit may be carried over to the following year, with certain exceptions.

Ultra-small emitters[25]

- **Eligibility.** An installation may qualify as an ultra-small emitter if it emits less than 2,500 tonnes of carbon dioxide equivalent annually. An application must be approved by both the firm's regulator and the ETS authority.

24 https://www.gov.uk/guidance/opt-out-of-the-uk-ets-if-your-installation-is-a-hospital-or-small-emitter

25 https://www.gov.uk/guidance/opt-out-of-the-uk-ets-if-your-installation-is-an-ultra-small-emitter

- **Benefits.** Ultra-small emitters may opt out of the ETS scheme entirely. They must still monitor their emissions and notify their regulator if emissions levels exceed an agreed-upon limit.

Units[26]

One UK ETS allowance credit allows its holder to emit one tonne of CO2 equivalent (CO2e). CO2e is a unit of measurement used to standardise the effects on the climate of various different GHG. Different GHG have a varying effect on climate and by using the CO2e the impact of each gas can be expressed in the amount of CO2 that would create the same warming effect. The UK Emissions Trading Registry acts as the central ledger for keeping track of credit ownership.

Free credits

Both installations and aircraft operators are provided with a certain number of **free credits**, calculated on a per-case basis and allocated on or before 28 February of each year. A full list of free allocations is published annually.[27] Free allocations are meant to act as a buffer to prevent sudden industry disruptions; their allocations are therefore meant to be reduced each year as industries adjust to the new system.

Auction system

As the free credit system is phased out, an **auction system** will serve as the primary means of introducing new credits to the market. Both ETS operators and financial institutions may bid in UK Allowance auctions but must register beforehand. Auctions are held every two weeks, with the volume of credits on auction determined in advance. The amount of

---

26 https://www.gov.uk/government/publications/taking-part-in-the-uk-emissions-trading-scheme-markets/taking-part-in-the-uk-emissions-trading-scheme-markets

27 https://www.gov.uk/government/publications/uk-ets-allocation-table-for-operators-of-installations

credits on auction has been trending down: 81m in 2022, 79m in 2023 and 69m in 2024. Credits left unsold in auction are redistributed across the subsequent four auctions, up to a certain threshold after which excess credits are transferred to a market stability mechanism account.

The credits sold on auction currently have a transitional Auction Reserve Price of £22; the government has specified that it will consult on its intent to withdraw the ARP at some point in the future. The auction clearing price is the price of the bid at which the sum of the volumes bid matches or exceeds the volume of allowances auctioned, subject to change if the price is significantly below secondary market prices.

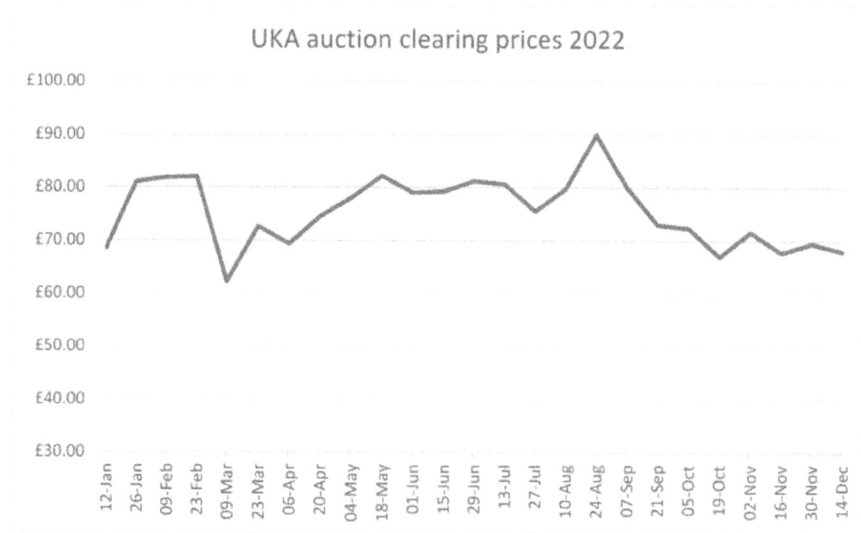

[28]

Secondary market

Market participants may trade credits via the Emissions Trading Registry. Price formation is over-the-counter; there is no central exchange. ICE

---

28 https://assets.publishing.service.gov.uk/government/uploads/system/uploads/attachment_data/file/1174408/functioning-of-the-uk-carbon-market.pdf

Futures Europe hosts a market for allowance credit derivatives such as futures contracts.

Cost Containment Mechanism[29]

The ETS framework includes a cost containment mechanism (CCM) which allows the government to intervene if credit prices remain elevated for a sustained period. The CCM is triggered if the monthly average end of day settlement price is three times the two-year average carbon price for 6 consecutive months. The final decision on what intervention to take is determined by HM Treasury, and can include increasing the volume of credits to be auctioned or redistributing credits between the current year's actions.

Voluntary Carbon Markets

Legal Framework

As a voluntary, decentralized system, there is no single authority or regulator overseeing the UK voluntary carbon market. Instead, there are a number of organizations that provide accreditation and standardization for each step of the transaction process.

- **Supply:** Landowners seeking to acquire carbon credits through use of their property may do so through accreditation programs. Which program depends on the type of land from which the credits are to be derived. At time of writing, the three main categories in the UK are woodland, peatland and soil; the individual processes will be outlined below. If the landowner's application is approved, they will then be issued carbon credits.

- **Marketplace:** With certified carbon credits in hand, the landowner must then find a buyer. Carbon credits are traded

[29] S 12 Greenhouse Gas Emissions Trading Scheme Auctioning Regulations 2021

"over the counter," meaning there is no central market like there is for stocks traded on listed exchanges. Instead, buyers and sellers must find each other and negotiate a price, either directly or via an intermediary who will connect buyers and sellers for a fee. Many regulated brokers provide such a service; alternatively, exchanges such as the London Stock Exchange provide platforms on which qualified market participants may place offers.

As the VCM space is unregulated, many market participants will seek third-party certification to verify that the environmental programs in which they are investing are making meaningful contributions to reducing the impact of global climate change. Non-profit organizations such as the Voluntary Carbon Markets Integrity Initiative[30] and the International Carbon Reduction & Offset Alliance[31] (ICROA) provide best practices and certify VCMs that adhere to such practices.

Landowner Carbon Credit Accreditation

Landowners may seek accreditation from different organizations depending on the land from which they seek to generate carbon credits.

Woodland

Woodland creation is the most common form of land use from which credits may be produced and is standardized by the Woodland Carbon Code (WCC). The WCC is managed by Scottish Forestry on behalf of the Forestry Commission[32] and endorsed by ICROA. Beyond selling on the open market, under the Woodland Carbon Guarantee scheme, WCC

30 https://vcmintegrity.org/

31 https://icroa.org/

32 https://woodlandcarboncode.org.uk/about/governance

units may also be sold to the UK government provided project developers applied for the option to do so before planting trees.[33]

Unit types[34]

Carbon credits are meant to equate to one tonne's worth of CO2e being removed from the atmosphere. For woodlands, this requires mature trees to capture the carbon, leading to an economic disincentive for landowners: why invest in planting woodland if they will not see returns for years to come? To tackle this issue, WCC programs issue two types of credits: Woodland Carbon Units (WCUs) and Pending Issuance Units (PIUs).

WCUs are verified credits representing one tonne of CO2e removed via woodland whereas PIUs represent a promise by the landowner to the buyer that the landowner will deliver a WCU by a certain date. PIUs are essentially a futures contract: they cannot be used to report against UK-based emissions, but they can effectively lock in use of a WCU at a future date for an agreed-upon price. PIU's can also be used as part of a firm's corporate social responsibility (CSR) commitments with regards to woodland creation.

Five years after initial validation and every ten years thereafter, independent auditors will inspect sites with PIUs and convert verified projects into WCUs.

Unit prices

As the WCC is a nascent project, over 99% of units transacted so far are PIUs. As of time of writing, the 2023 volume-weighted average price (VWAP) of one PIU is £25.36, up 33% year-on-year from the 2022

33 https://woodlandcarboncode.org.uk/landowners-apply/how-do-i-sell-my-carbon-units

34 https://www.woodlandcarboncode.org.uk/buy-carbon/what-are-woodland-carbon-units

VWAP of £19.13.[35] A native woodland generates approximately 400 units per hectare, meaning at 2023 prices a hectare of woodland would generate approximately £10,144 in carbon credit revenues annually. Income from commercial forestry is not subject to income or corporation tax.[36]

	2021	2022	2023*
Transaction Volume	233,022	212,275	60,355
Hi-Lo Spread	£27.76	£33.20	£37.50
PIU VWAP (Nominal)	£14.93	£19.13	£25.36
PIU VWAP (Real)	£15.74	£19.13	£24.15

*Source: Woodland Carbon Code * as of June 2023*

As mentioned previously, approved projects may also sell their WCUs to the UK government via the Woodland Carbon Guarantee.[37] The programme was launched in November 2019 with a budget of £50m to be spent over 30 years. The price at which the government purchases units is determined via auction. Auctions are hosted on an ad-hoc basis; as of writing, seven auctions have been hosted.

35 https://woodlandcarboncode.org.uk/uk-land-carbon-registry/uk-carbon-prices

36 https://woodlandcarboncode.org.uk/landowners-apply/benefits-to-landowners

37 https://woodlandcarboncode.org.uk/woodland-carbon-guarantee

	Total bids	Successful bids	Area successful bids (ha)	Avg. price of successful bids (weighted by no of WCU)
Auction 1: 2020	31	18	182	£24.11
Auction 2: 2020	77	27	1,517	£19.71
Auction 3: 2020	46	31	620	£17.31
Auction 4: 2021	23	19	331	£18.62
Auction 5: 2022	16	15	99	£23.70
Auction 6: 2022	9	9	59	£22.61
Auction 7: 2023	2	2		£19.76

Source: Woodland Carbon Code

Process

1. **Planning.**[38] Develop a Woodland Carbon project strategy. This can be done either alone or with the support of a project

[38] https://woodlandcarboncode.org.uk/landowners-apply/1-need-help-find-a-project-developer

developer that will help you through the process. The WCC website includes a list of potential project developers.

2. **Registration.** Create an account with the UK Land Carbon Registry. This can be done online.

3. **Submission.**[39] Projects can be submitted either alone or as part of a group. Registering as a group would allow smaller woodland owners to share administrative burdens and lower overall costs. Your strategy must include:

    a. The project name and description

    b. Project implementation date (when work begins), start date (when planting ends), and end date (up to 100 years after start date)

    c. Management regime

    d. Validator

    e. Location

    f. Net Area

    g. Predicted carbon sequestration over project lifetime

    h. Draft carbon calculations

    i. A map

4. **Validation.**[40] Once your strategy is approved, it will need to be validated by an accredited validation body. You will have three

39 https://woodlandcarboncode.org.uk/landowners-apply/2-register-your-project

40 https://woodlandcarboncode.org.uk/landowners-apply/3-validation-initial-project-check

years from registration to validate the project. Validation cannot be completed until all trees are planted, but the process can be started in parallel with plantation. Validation costs between £1,100 and £1,400 per project. A project that undergoes significant changes after validation will need to be revalidated. Once validated, the landowner will be issued PIUs which they can sell.

5. **Ongoing verification.**[41] A project will need to undergo regular inspection to ensure that the woodland is being developed in line with the approved strategy. The first verification occurs five years after the project is validated and every ten years thereafter. During these inspections, the inspectors will also calculate how much carbon has been captured by the project so far and will convert PIUs into WCUs accordingly. Landowners may also conduct self-assessments, however without third-party inspection PIUs cannot be converted into WCUs.[42]

Peatland

Peatlands are a type of wetland in which accumulated dead plant material is prevented from degrading due to water saturation. This layer of plant material—known as peat—captures and sequesters carbon. Peatlands are the world's largest store of land-based carbon: despite making up only 3% of the world's surface, peatlands hold 30% of the world's soil carbon—double the carbon stored in global forests.[43]

Unfortunately, unsuitable land management practices have damaged much of the UK's peatlands, causing them to release their stored carbon

41 https://woodlandcarboncode.org.uk/landowners-apply/4-verification-ongoing-check-of-project-sequestration

42 https://woodlandcarboncode.org.uk/landowners-apply/5-self-assessment

43 https://www.iucn-uk-peatlandprogramme.org/about-peatlands

at around 20m tonnes of CO2e each year—about 4% of the UK's total emissions.[44]

The Peatland Code[45] was established to tackle this issue by providing carbon credits to landowners seeking to restore eroded peatland. The Code was published in 2017 and updated in 2023 by the IUCN UK National Committee; it serves as a process through which restored peatland may accumulate carbon credits provided the land meets the required conditions. The process for registering for such credits is nearly identical to the Woodland Carbon Code process: PIUs are issued at the project's onset, which are eventually transformed into Peatland Carbon Units (PCUs) following verification by a third party.

Unit Prices

As a nascent project, no PIUs have yet to be converted into PCUs, so all price data is for PIUs. 11,416 credits were traded in 2022 with a volume weighted average price (VWAP) of £23.95 with a £25.00 spread between the highest and lowest reported price.[46] There has so far been insufficient reported data to provide figures for 2023.

Process

As mentioned, the process for developing a peatland project is similar to that of a woodland project:

---

44 https://uk-air.defra.gov.uk/assets/documents/reports/cat07/1904111135_UK_peatland_GHG_emissions.pdf

45 https://www.iucn-uk-peatlandprogramme.org/sites/default/files/2023-03/Peatland%20Code%20V2%20-%20FINAL%20-%20WEB_0.pdf

46 https://www.iucn-uk-peatlandprogramme.org/peatland-code/uk-carbon-price-index

1. **Planning.**[47] Ensure that your project is eligible. Landowners may choose to work with developers to ensure project compliance; the peatland code website provides a list of developers with active Peatland Code projects.[48] Basic pre-requisites are set out by the Peatland Code, and include (at time of writing):

    - Peat soils must be greater than 30cm in depth for bogs with additional requirements, 45cm in fens
    - Peatland type must be blanket, raised bog or fen
    - Peatland condition must be 'Actively Eroding', 'Drained', 'Modified bog', 'Cropland – drained', 'Grassland – intensive', 'Grassland – extensive' or 'Modified fen'
    - Restoration activities must not include forestry removal
    - Restoration must not be legally or contractually required
    - Project must be able to enter a minimum contract of 30 years
    - Restoration activities must not conflict with any other land management agreements
    - Project must be additional i.e. it must require carbon finance to take place

---

47 https://www.iucn-uk-peatlandprogramme.org/peatland-code/introduction-peatland-code/projects

48 https://www.iucn-uk-peatlandprogramme.org/peatland-code/useful-project-design-contacts

2. **Registration.** Create an account with the UK Land Carbon Registry. This can be done online.[49]

3. **Submission.** Complete a field survey of the project site and submit the necessary documentation. The required documents can be found on the Peatland Code website.[50]

4. **Validation.** Secure validation of your project by a third party. As of writing, there are only three bodies approved to validate Peatland Code projects: Organic Farmers & Growers (OF&G), Soil Association and SAC Consulting. [51] PIUs may be issued at this step.

5. **Ongoing verification.** The project must first arrange for third-party verification within one year of finishing restoration activities to ensure the project has followed its submitted restoration plan. If PIUs were issued at step 4, they may be adjusted at this step. Projects must then arrange for verification five years after validation, and every ten years thereafter. PIUs are converted into PCUs following each verification.

49 https://www.iucn-uk-peatlandprogramme.org/sites/default/files/2020-11/UK%20Land%20Carbon%20Registry%20User%20Guide_30November2020.pdf

50 https://www.iucn-uk-peatlandprogramme.org/peatland-code/introduction-peatland-code/projects

51 Ibid.

CHAPTER THREE

BIODIVERSITY

Global context

All habitats on Earth rely on a delicate balance of plants and animals to survive. Small changes to one element of a biosphere—redirecting a waterway, for example—can produce a domino effect that could lead to a fundamental alteration or destruction of a natural habitat with potentially global consequences. Governments around the world are developing legislation to try and address this issue without causing unnecessary harm to economic development.

England context

Each country within the UK has taken a different approach towards regulation, with England having developed a credit-based "Biodiversity Net Gain" (BNG) system outlined below. The position in Scotland, Wales and Northern Ireland is discussed in Chapter 10.

<u>Objective</u>[52]

- The principle of BNG forms part of the government's 25-year plan on the environment for England – to leave it in a better state than we found it.

- When applying for **planning permission**, applicants must **submit a plan detailing how the proposed development will increase biodiversity by at least 10%.**

[52] Michelmores, Biodiversity Net Gain: The Basics, https://www.michelmores.com/agriculture-insight/biodiversity-net-gain-basics/ (26.04.22)

- Individual local planning authorities will have the power to set higher percentage thresholds should they wish.

The Environment Act 2021 (the Act) received Royal Assent on 9 November 2021 and introduces a mandatory 10% BNG requirement in England for all developments under the Town and Country Planning Act 1990 (TCPA), with very limited exceptions.

The Act follows the existing BNG policy requirement in the National Planning Policy Framework. Schedule 14 of the Act (link) inserts a new schedule into the TCPA requiring applicants to submit a biodiversity gain plan at the planning application stage. The plan must detail how the development will meet the minimum 10% BNG requirement; however, the 10% is a minimum requirement, and individual local planning authorities ("**LPAs**") have the power to set higher percentage thresholds should they wish.

Terminology

Before going into the detail it would be helpful to first clarify a couple of points which relate to the contents of this chapter.

The government definition of "biodiversity credits" is unhelpfully wide as there are more than one type of biodiversity credit: statutory biodiversity credits and biodiversity credits derived from registered offsite gains and traded on the private market.

- **Statutory Credits:** The Act and associated guidance refers to "biodiversity credits"[53] by which it means statutory credits which can be purchased from the Secretary of State at a price set by the government. This, as will be explained later in this chapter, is a last resort for developers where all other onsite and offsite options

[53] Section 101 of the Environment Act 2021

have been exhausted. Such credits will be referred to as "statutory credits" throughout the book.

- **Offsite Credits:** Unlike statutory credits, offsite biodiversity credits are traded on the private market. This term will apply equally to all registered offsite gains, whether they are direct deals done between developers and landowners or via an intermediary such as a broker or habitat banker.

The biodiversity of a site is calculated via the **Biodiversity Metric**, a standardized statutory framework whose output is measured in **Biodiversity Units**. DEFRA provides a biodiversity metric calculation tool and a comprehensive user guide which explains how Biodiversity Units are calculated.[54] These units are then converted into tradeable Offsite Credits. That conversion is achieved by the combined operation of a credit purchase agreement and section 106 agreement/conservation covenant. The former creates and transfers the Offsite Credit, and the latter underwrites the value and validity of the same.

A developer may create Biodiversity Units within the redline of their development site, then if the gain is insufficient to meet the 10% gain threshold they may purchase Offsite Credits and Statutory Credits until it has enough credits to submit a Biodiversity Gain Plan. If, on the other hand, a developer has a surplus of on-site Biodiversity Units, for example as a result of habitat creation work on its development site, then it may sell those excess units as Offsite Credits to another developer.

54 https://www.gov.uk/government/publications/statutory-biodiversity-metric-tools-and-guides

Secondary Legislation

In January 2024, the government published secondary BNG legislation which fleshed out the bones of the Environment Act 2021. These new statutory instruments required mandatory BNG for all new planning applications made post 12 February 2024.

- The Biodiversity Gain Site Register Regulations 2024 (Draft) ("**Register Regulations**") (https://www.gov.uk/government/publications/the-biodiversity-gain-site-register-regulations-2024)

- The Biodiversity Gain Site Register (Financial Penalties and Fees) Regulations 2024 ("**Fees Regulations**") (https://www.legislation.gov.uk/uksi/2024/46/contents/made)

- The Biodiversity Gain Requirements (Exemptions) Regulations 2024 ("**Exemptions Regulations**") (https://www.legislation.gov.uk/uksi/2024/47/contents/made)

- The Biodiversity Gain Requirements (Irreplaceable Habitat) Regulations 2024 ("**Irreplaceable Habitats Regulations**") (https://www.legislation.gov.uk/uksi/2024/48/contents/made)

- The Biodiversity Gain (Town and Country Planning) (Consequential Amendments) Regulations 2024 ("**Amendments Regulations**") (https://www.legislation.gov.uk/uksi/2024/49/contents/made)

- The Biodiversity Gain (Town and Country Planning) (Modifications and Amendments) (England) Regulations 2024 ("**Modifications Regulations**") (https://www.legislation.gov.uk/uksi/2024/50/contents/made)

As mentioned, the Environment Act 2021 introduced a mandatory 10% BNG requirement in England for **all developments** under the Town and

Country Planning Act 1990, with very limited exceptions. This requirement was meant to come into effect in November 2023 (April 2024 for smaller sites), but this deadline was postponed to 12 February 2024.

<u>Quantifying BNG</u>

The BNG objective is met in relation to development if the biodiversity value attributable to it exceeds the pre-development biodiversity value by at least 10%. The biodiversity value attributable to development is a total of:

- the post-development biodiversity value of the onsite habitat;
- the biodiversity value of any registered offsite biodiversity gain allocated to the development; and
- the biodiversity value of any Biodiversity Credits (Offsite and Statutory) purchased for the development.

This means that the first task for a developer is to assess the pre-development biodiversity value of the development site so that they can quantify their BNG requirement. This, like other calculations of biodiversity, is achieved via the Biodiversity Metric provided by DEFRA. An assessment is required of the biodiversity which will be lost as a result of the development works and any mitigation achieved through onsite provision.

The relevant date for the pre-development calculation is the date of submission of the planning application, unless the site has suffered from unauthorised environmental degradation, in which case the date will be 30 January 2020. This is to ensure that landowners do not artificially lower the biodiversity value of their sites before calculating their starting BNG figure so as to more easily achieve the 10% gain threshold. Details of what constitutes "unauthorized environmental degradation" will be discussed later in this chapter.

The BNG requirement may be achieved through a combination of three routes:

- **onsite provision**: the developer is able to enhance biodiversity directly on the development site.
- **offsite provision**: developers may allocate habitat creation on another site they control or purchase Offsite Credits from other market participants to offset biodiversity loss incurred by the development. This has led to the development of "habitat banks," developments designed to maximise Biodiversity Units and sell the excess units on the market.
- **statutory credits:** If developers are unable to secure sufficient Offsite Credits via on- and off-site provisions, they may as a last resort make up the difference via the purchase of Statutory Credits from the UK government; however, these credits are sold at a premium to ensure that the private market for Offsite Credits is not distorted and the developer must show that it has exhausted all other methods of achieving the biodiversity objective.

Developing onsite BNG might not be attractive for many developers as the area could be better utilised for other purposes or more profitably used for development. As such, offsite BNG provision is a rapidly developing space and the use of habitat banks is becoming more commonplace. Developers may also start optioning larger areas of land to factor in the provision of BNG in the future.

Mitigation & BNG Hierarchy

When considering their options, developers have a positive obligation to follow a hierarchy of actions to mitigate biodiversity reduction: first, to avoid biodiversity loss; if impossible, then minimise it, then mitigate the effects of the development; and finally if all the above is impossible then offset or compensate for any loss.

In practice, this means a developer should, in order of priority:

1. Aim to **avoid or reduce biodiversity impacts** through site selection and layout

2. **Enhance and restore biodiversity** on site

3. **Create or enhance offsite habitats**, either on their land or by purchasing Offsite Credits

4. **Purchase Statutory Credits** as a last resort

While this mitigation hierarchy is well established, a **new biodiversity gain hierarchy** has also been introduced by the Modifications Regulations[55] which provides a variation on the avoid, minimise, compensate and offset theme. The biodiversity gain hierarchy firstly distinguishes between development sites which have onsite habitat with a **habitat distinctiveness score** (as calculated via the Biodiversity Metric) of four or higher from those whose score does not meet such a threshold.

Distinctiveness Category	Distinctiveness Score
Very high	8
High	6
Medium	4
Low	2

Source: DEFRA Statutory Biodiversity Metric User Guide

[55] Part 4 of The Biodiversity Gain (Town and Country Planning) (Modifications and Amendments) (England) Regulations 2024 inserts new Articles 37A – E into the Town and Country Planning (Development Management Procedure) (England) Order 2015

The biodiversity gain hierarchy will therefore only apply to sites with this habitat of medium distinctiveness or above. Sites with a score at or above the threshold must, in order of priority:

- **avoid** adverse effects of the development on onsite habitat with a habitat distinctiveness score equal to or higher than four;
- so far as those adverse effects cannot be avoided, **mitigate** those effects.

On sites where the habitat distinctiveness score is less than four, there is no obligation to avoid adverse effects of development with a requirement to simply enhance or create onsite habitat. However, sites below the threshold will need to have the standard mitigation hierarchy applied which in any event forms part of the National Planning Policy Framework.[56]

This means that, in relation to **any** such onsite habitat (irrespective of habitat distinctiveness score) adversely affected by development, developers must compensate for that adverse effect by:

- **Mitigating** any adverse effects;
- if those adverse effects cannot be mitigated, **enhance** onsite habitats;
- if further enhancement of existing habitats is impossible, **create** additional onsite habitats;
- if no further habitats can be created, **secure offsite credits**;
- so far as that offsite habitat enhancement cannot be secured, purchase **statutory credits**.

[56] Paragraph 186 of the National Planning Policy Framework

Developers are encouraged to follow the biodiversity gain and/or the standard mitigation hierarchies from the earliest stage possible when selecting a site and considering development proposals.

Local planning authorities must take into account the use of these hierarchies when considering whether the biodiversity objective has been met and when determining whether to approve the Biodiversity Gain Plan.

What these hierarchies mean for developers

DEFRA has been clear that all three options in the mitigation hierarchy (onsite, offsite, statutory) can be combined; developers are free to meet their BNG targets by buying credits from a habitat broker or doing a private deal on nearby land.

The guidance does say that "buying statutory credits means that as well as, or instead of, creating and enhancing biodiversity on or off a development site, developers can make a financial contribution which counts towards their mandatory 10% BNG."[57] Ultimately, a developer may be able to meet their BNG requirement by statutory credits alone if on site and off site are both ruled out.

However, **ultimately approval remains up to the discretion of LPAs**, and given LPA autonomy these authorities may all have different approaches to the biodiversity gain hierarchy. Some may apply the rules with greater rigour than others in requiring developers to show that onsite options are not available. What might seem reasonable to a developer may not meet with the LPA's approval. There may be very good economic reasons why the density of housing units has to be at a certain level, but such density could nonetheless conflict with environmental arguments such as maintaining a distinctive habitat. As with issues like affordable housing provision or section 106 contributions, these issues will have to be

57 https://www.gov.uk/guidance/statutory-biodiversity-credits#overview

negotiated in the usual manner and a compromise reached so as to allow sustainable development to proceed.

Biodiversity Units: Market Size and Market Participants

Employing a working assumption that 50% of biodiversity net gain would be delivered off-site, a DEFRA report estimates an annual offsite demand of 6,200 biodiversity units with an estimated value of £135m.[58]

It is hard to predict the size of the Offsite Credit market as doing so requires assessing to what extent developers will be able or willing to provide habitat as part of their development schemes. The mitigation hierarchy clearly encourages developers to prioritise on-site solutions. The spatial multipliers in the Biodiversity Metric also feed into the golden thread of biodiversity net gain, which is mitigating damage as close as possible to the development which caused it.

One potential influence on market size is the actions of LPAs offering Offsite Credits which have been generated from land within their ownership or control. The Localism Act 2011 gives LPAs substantial discretion to act commercially, but there is clearly potential for a conflict of interest when the LPA is both decision maker in a planning context and also a potential provider of Offsite Credits. Any LPA will likely have to have a transparent decision-making process in terms of considering applications from developers that have chosen to purchase third-party Offsite Credits over those belonging to the LPA. The decision will have to be justified on the basis of clear planning and environmental principles – proximity to development and strategic location in terms of Local Nature Recovery Strategies ("**LNRS**") are likely to be factors given considerable weight.

There are also issues for LPAs in terms of them acting as Responsible Bodies and/or attempting to contract with themselves in terms of section

[58] https://greenfinanceobservatory.org/wp-content/uploads/2022/06/UK-Biodiversity-Unit-Market-2.0-1.pdf

106 agreements. An LPA cannot be the party obliged to create/maintain habitat and be the enforcing authority in respect of the same. Although there are ways of getting around these contractual issues this is another potential conflict of interest they will have to negotiate.

Statutory Credits

Statutory Credits are a last resort and are priced[59] deliberately high so as not to distort the private market. Prices will be reviewed every six months and any planned changes will be trailed with at least 10 weeks' notice.

Statutory Credits are priced relative to the development site's habitat distinctiveness, which is grouped in categories of low, medium and high. Low distinctiveness habitats of all types are the cheapest at £42,000. The prices then increase according to the habitat type and distinctiveness. The cheaper end of the range is grassland, cropland, urban, individual trees and the more expensive are the rarer wetland, peatland and coastal habitats.

Statutory Credits are also subject to a 'spatial risk multiplier' of 2x, which means two Statutory Credits must be purchased for every one missing Biodiversity Unit. The Biodiversity Metric will automatically calculate this multiplication. This is meant to ensure that Statutory Credits do not compete with Offsite Credits and remain a last resort.

This effectively means that for the most basic habitat the final Statutory Credit price could be four or five times that being charged in the private market.

As soon as the developer identifies a shortfall necessitating the purchase of Statutory Credits, it should discuss this as part of their overall strategy with the relevant LPA. The developer will be required to prove to the

59 https://www.gov.uk/guidance/statutory-biodiversity-credit-prices

LPA that they need to buy the Statutory Credits. This is done by providing both of the following pieces of evidence:

- The developer has considered additional on-site BNG and can provide reasoning showing why this is not possible; and
- The developer has approached three local or national suppliers, habitat banks or trading websites and can show evidence that no off-site options are available in England.

Evidence of the lack of offsite options would include, for example, correspondence, emails, or a PDF download showing a marketplace search.

If a developer needs less than 0.25 biodiversity units (area or linear), they can buy Statutory Credits without needing to show evidence that no off-site options are available. However, the developer will still need to provide evidence that on-site BNG is insufficient to meet the requirements.

When the LPA is satisfied that the developer is eligible to purchase Statutory Credits, they should confirm this.

Once confirmed and the developer is satisfied they can discharge all other pre-commencement planning conditions, it can purchase the necessary Statutory Credits. The purchase should happen as late as possible in the planning process.

Due diligence checks will be carried out and then the invoice will be sent to the developer. Once the developer pays, it will receive a combined proof of purchase and VAT receipt. The developer needs to provide this proof of purchase with their Biodiversity Gain Plan. They must also submit to the LPA a biodiversity metric calculation that shows how they will meet their mandatory BNG.

Statutory Credits are linked to the planning reference number and Biodiversity Gain Plan for which they have been purchased. They cannot be transferred to other planning permissions or gain plans.

If a developer sells land with a planning permission and approved Biodiversity Gain Plan for which they have purchased Statutory Credits, the new owner may be able to benefit from the credits if they wish to proceed with the planning permission.

Natural England sells Statutory Credits on behalf of DEFRA. Proceeds from the sale of credits will be invested in habitat creation or enhancement, as set out in the Act.

Biodiversity Gain Plan

Under the statutory framework for biodiversity net gain, every grant of planning permission is deemed to have been granted subject to a general biodiversity gain condition to secure the biodiversity gain objective.

This objective is to deliver at least a 10% increase in relation to the pre-development biodiversity value of the development site relating to the permission. As set out above, this increase can be achieved through onsite biodiversity gains, Offsite Credits or Statutory Credits.

In terms of timing, the general biodiversity gain condition is a pre-commencement condition: once planning permission has been granted, a Biodiversity Gain Plan must be submitted by the developer and approved by the planning authority before commencement of the development.

There are exemptions and transitional arrangements which disapply the condition from certain planning permissions, as well as special modifications for planning permissions for phased development and the treatment of irreplaceable habitats.

The developer can submit the biodiversity gain plan to the relevant LPA after the planning application has been approved. This can lead to a "chicken and egg" issue in terms of timing, as developers may want the certainty of having secured planning permission before purchasing Statutory or Offsite Credits, while LPAs will want assurance of a project meeting BNG requirements before issuing planning permission. Developers may resolve this impasse by agreeing to a credit purchase agreement. The agreement would secure the right to buy the Offsite Credits once the planning permission has been secured in exchange for a small deposit. The balance can then be paid when the credits are drawn down so as to demonstrate compliance with the general biodiversity gain condition by the submission of a valid biodiversity gain plan.

Every applicable planning permission will include a general biodiversity gain condition, so the development cannot be commenced until the LPA approves the biodiversity gain plan and Biodiversity Metric calculation.

Once a biodiversity gain plan is submitted, the LPA has eight weeks to approve or refuse the plan. Once their plan is approved, the developer will have discharged their general biodiversity gain condition.

If the developer does not meet the BNG requirements, the LPA can take enforcement action as the developer will be in breach of planning conditions and/or obligations.

Developers must also complete a biodiversity gain plan template. There are different templates for:

- Major developments and small sites; and
- Phased developments

Biodiversity Gain Plan Requirements

Developers need to provide their:

- Completed Biodiversity Metric calculation

- Pre-development and post-development plans (showing the location of on-site habitat, the direction of north and drawn to an identified scale)

Developers must also provide:

- A compensation plan if the development affects irreplaceable habitats
- Biodiversity net gain register reference numbers for any off-site units
- Proof of purchase for any Statutory Credits
- A habitat management and monitoring plan for off-site or significant on-site gains

Pre-development biodiversity value start date

Paragraph 5 of Schedule 7A[60] sets out that the 'relevant date' used to calculate the pre-development biodiversity value of the onsite habitat as either:

- where planning permission is granted on application, the date of the application; or
- in any other case, the date on which the planning permission is granted.

The person submitting the Biodiversity Gain Plan for approval and the LPA may agree that the relevant date is an earlier date, but this cannot be a date which is before the day on which Schedule 7A came into force in relation to the development.

60 Town and Country Planning Act 1990

In order to ensure an accurate pre-development biodiversity calculation, surveys of the development site should ideally be done shortly before the submission of the planning application. Older surveys can be used where there has been no material change to the onsite habitat when the planning application is submitted.

As part of the planning application form, an applicant will need to identify the proposed relevant date and, if this proposed date will be an earlier date than the date of the planning application, identify the reasons why. This will help inform the agreement of an earlier date between the person submitting the Biodiversity Gain Plan and the LPA.

Applicants are encouraged to engage with the LPA prior to submitting the planning application to discuss the use of or need for an earlier date, in order to avoid potential disputes later.

Once permission has been granted, the relevant date will also need to be set out in the Biodiversity Gain Plan.

Pre-development habitat degradation

There are special provisions for the calculation of the pre-development biodiversity value of onsite habitat when habitat degradation has occurred prior to the submission of a planning application in order to discourage the deliberate degradation of existing habitats to reduce the pre-development biodiversity value.

Where degradation of onsite habitats has taken place before the application is submitted, the relevant date should be an earlier date immediately before the degradation occurred.

Where unauthorised degradation of the onsite habitat has taken place between 30 January 2020 and the date of the submission of the planning application, the biodiversity pre-development value of the onsite habitat is the biodiversity value of the habitat immediately before the carrying out of these degradation activities. The relevant date should therefore be set as a date immediately before these activities. Unauthorised degradation of onsite habitat is any degradation which is not in accordance with a previous planning permission.

If there has been unauthorised degradation and there is insufficient evidence about the biodiversity value of the onsite habitat immediately before the degradation, the pre-development biodiversity value of the onsite habitat must be taken to be the highest biodiversity value of the habitat which is reasonably supported by any available evidence relating to it. This requirement must be applied to the calculation of pre-development biodiversity value in the Biodiversity Metric, and the Biodiversity Gain Plan template asks for information regarding whether there has been prior habitat degradation.

The maintenance of a significant onsite habitat enhancement must be secured by either a planning condition, planning obligation or conservation covenant.

Timings of Onsite vs Offsite solutions

It is useful to pause here and focus on the different requirements for onsite and offsite solutions. If a developer is meeting their BNG objective partially or completely through onsite habitat provision then the requirement is to maintain that habitat **for at least 30 years after the completion of the development.**[61]

This obligation is different from the offsite situation which requires habitat maintenance for 30 years starting from **the completion of the habitat enhancement works.**[62]

This raises several issues in terms of legal drafting and practical habitat management; these issues are discussed briefly below.

61 Paragraph 9 (3) of Schedule 7A of the Town and Country Planning Act 1990

62 Section 100 of the Environment Act 2021.

The first is that the completion date of the development may be difficult to pin down particularly where some or all of the work is phased albeit that phasing of development can be specifically matched to the BNG requirements – see later. If development is not commenced for a significant period of time, then there may not be the required 30 year run-off left in the BNG agreements. This risk can, of course, be mitigated by providing for, say, 32-year leases or agreements, but it is a point to bear in mind when drafting and agreeing Heads of Terms.

Another issue is that whilst the completion of development is easy to understand in conceptual terms, the "*completion of habitat enhancement works*" is a bit more nebulous. There will not always be a clear demarcation between the completion of habitat creation/enhancement works and their subsequent maintenance. For these purposes, there appears to be no distinction between habitat creation and enhancement, with the latter being used as a catch all phrase in section 100 of the Act.

It might be helpful to think in terms of what would be regarded as initial capital type works under stewardship schemes such as planting of habitat and any necessary clearance or cultivation works. When drafting documents, drawing a "line in the sand" after such works can be useful as it clarifies which projects are regarded as the habitat enhancement works. Anything that follows is maintenance and the 30 year clock starts accordingly.

In an attempt to avoid such problems with onsite provision, the guidance states that when setting such conditions the LPA should work with applicants to clearly establish the point of completion after which the 30 year period begins. The definition of completion should include the completion of any onsite habitat enhancements (not just the buildings related to the development) which would constitute development.

As these projects are in relation to habitat enhancement works, the use of traditional indicators of completion for residential or commercial development (such as a building regulations notice) should be not relied on for the formal 'completion' of the development (i.e. when the final unit is completed) for the purposes of these provisions.

In drawing together their biodiversity gain plans, developers will then have to assess the post-development biodiversity value, which will take into account the effects of the development and any positive effect caused by green space being incorporated within the development (such as Suitable Alternative Natural Greenspace (SANG) land).

Onsite BNG Provision

What remains unclear is to what extent any onsite BNG provision supplied by developers will need to be on the BNG Register.

"Registered Offsite Biodiversity Gain" relates to enhancement of habitat recorded in the BNG Register.[63] This omits onsite provision from the requirements and scrutiny of the BNG Register and nothing in the Register Regulations remedies that.

Any such onsite provision may well be delivered through the mechanism of a section 106 agreement or conservation covenant and generally meet the eligibility criteria for site registration set out in Regulation 6[64].

Onsite BNG provision supplied by developers does not need to be registered on the BNG Register nor allocated, but significant onsite gains must still be secured legally for at least 30 years after the development is completed. The government has said it is exploring how onsite information can be extracted from planning permission and published on the BNG Register so that all BNG information, whether onsite or offsite, is accessible in one place.

---

63 Paragraph 10 of Schedule 7A of the Town and Country Planning Act 1990

64 Biodiversity Gain Site Register Regulations 2024

It does not seem unreasonable to subject onsite BNG to the same level of scrutiny as offsite, as the two need to be of an equivalent standard.

Phased Development

The statutory framework for biodiversity net gain includes specific modifications for planning permissions (including outline permissions) that have the effect of permitting development in phases. This reflects how phased development can occur over a long period of time and that full details of all phases may not be known at the time of planning permission. For these permissions, the standard approach for Biodiversity Gain Plan approval which must include details of significant onsite habitats enhancements, allocated registered offsite gains and the purchase of biodiversity credits is not possible. For the purposes of biodiversity net gain, a phased development is a development where there is:

- a grant of outline planning permission where the reservation of matters for subsequent approval has the effect of requiring or permitting development to proceed in phases; or

- a grant of any kind of planning permission, where the grant is subject to conditions (whether requiring the subsequent approval of any matters or otherwise) having that effect.

An example of a phased development would be a largescale urban extension for residential or commercial development where an outline planning permission has been granted, and the permission identifies clear phases for development where subsequent reserved matter approvals would grant consent for the detailed design of a phase.

Not all outline planning permissions will meet this different definition. For instance, an outline permission for a small-scale residential development where appearance and landscaping were the only reserved matters for later determination is unlikely to fall into this category, and would therefore be subject to the standard provisions for biodiversity net gain.

The planning permission decision notice for a development will indicate whether the development is phased for the purposes of biodiversity net gain, and therefore the development would be subject to specific provisions for phased development.

What are the modifications for phased development?

The Modifications Regulations modify the general biodiversity condition for planning permissions which are in respect of phased development. Phased developments require two plans:

- an **Overall Biodiversity Gain Plan** must be submitted to and approved by the planning authority before any development can begin; and

- a **Phase Biodiversity Gain Plan** for each phase must be submitted to and approved by the planning authority before the development of that phase can begin.

In recognition that phased development can often be implemented over a long period of time, the purpose of the Overall Biodiversity Gain Plan is to set a clear upfront framework for how the biodiversity gain objective of at least a 10% gain is expected to be met across the entire development. Each Phase Biodiversity Gain Plan will subsequently set out a phase's biodiversity contribution and track progress towards the overall biodiversity gain objective for the development once clear proposals for each phase have been developed. It is envisaged that, for an outline planning permission for phased development, the Phase Biodiversity Gain Plan would be prepared alongside the application for reserve matter approvals for a phase.

How is an Overall Biodiversity Gain Plan different from a standard Biodiversity Gain Plan?

Unlike a standard Biodiversity Gain Plan for a non-phased project, the content of an Overall Biodiversity Gain Plan will reflect that certain details for significant onsite habitat enhancements, especially for later phases, have yet to be determined, and that offsite gains and credits might not be allocated or purchased for the development immediately.

The Overall Biodiversity Gain Plan for a phased development (which is not a section 73 permission) must include the following matters:

- information about the steps taken or to be taken to minimise the adverse effect of the development on the biodiversity of the onsite habitat and any other habitat;
- the pre-development biodiversity value of the entire onsite habitat;
- any registered offsite biodiversity gain proposed to be allocated to the entire development and the biodiversity value of that gain in relation to the development;
- any biodiversity credits proposed to be purchased for the entire development; and
- the strategy for meeting the biodiversity gain objective if there is a change to the post-development biodiversity value, proposed registered offsite biodiversity gain or proposed purchase of biodiversity credits.

The post-development biodiversity value of the onsite habitat is an estimate of the value at the completion of the entire development, not the individual phases leading to completion. Where firm proposals for development and habitat enhancement on each phase have yet to be finalised, assumptions about the likely development and habitat enhancements should be used to determine this post-development value. This value will set the expectations about the biodiversity value of onsite habitats and deviations will need to be justified in later Phase Biodiversity Gain Plans.

BNG registration and enforcement

The Register Regulations require Natural England to set up and maintain a centralized repository of all BNG sites; applicants will have to ensure their site is properly registered in order to qualify for BNG credits. The repository will be accessible to the public.

- **Who can apply.** Only the person required to carry out or maintain the habitat enhancement or a person who can enforce the requirement may apply to register land.[65]
    - Bodies responsible under a conservation covenant may not apply to register land in relation to that covenant.[66]
- **Land eligibility.** For land to be registered, a section 106 agreement (a legal agreement between a planning authority and the landowner) or a conservation covenant must be in place.[67]
    - A section 106 agreement or a conservation covenant may only be registered once.[68]
    - It is possible for the same land to be registered more than once (see below in terms of initial registration of a wider area of land and then subsequent allocation to a development).[69]

65 Regulation 7(2) Biodiversity Gain Site Register Regulations 2024 (Draft)

66 Regulation 7(3)

67 Regulation 5(1)

68 Regulation 5(2)

69 Regulation 12

- The habitat enhancement must include a 30-year maintenance period and linked to a particular development.[70]

    - We have been careful to distinguish, when drafting agreements, between the initial works of habitat establishment/enhancement and their subsequent maintenance for at least 30 years.

- The habitat must be monitored to ensure it is being properly maintained and on track to achieving the desired outcome.[71]

    - The question of who monitors the delivery of the habitat enhancement works and who pays for that has been the subject of negotiation on some deals. That issue is now decided (although already surely inherent in the landowner's overall obligation to enhance the habitat successfully) in that a person must be obliged to do so by the section 106 agreement or conservation covenant. The question of monitoring costs is one for commercial negotiation between the landowner and developer. There is a clear overlap between landowners monitoring their habitat and LPAs keeping an eye on a site with a view to enforcement of a section 106 agreement.

- **Applications.**[72] All claims made by the application must be substantiated (e.g. the applicant's ability to make the claim and the eligibility of the land and improvement in question). This includes all relevant licences and permissions required to deliver

---

70 Regulation 6(3)

71 Regulation 6(4)

72 Regulation 8

the improvement. Where improvement work has already begun, applicants must include documentation on the condition of the habitat before the work began.

- An application to register land under a conservation covenant **may only be made by the person required to carry out or maintain works** of habitat enhancement or, pursuant to regulation 7(2)(c), a person who can enforce a requirement to deliver or maintain those works.
    - This broadly places the application responsibilities on the landowner and regulation 7(3) expressly forbids a responsible body under a conservation covenant from making such an application.
- If **section 106 agreements are being used**, then an application to register land may only be made by the person required to carry out or maintain works of habitat enhancement.
- If **section 106 agreements are not being used**, then an application to register land under a conservation covenant may only be made by the person required to carry out or maintain works of habitat enhancement.

- **Content of Applications.**[73] The detail required here is, unsurprisingly, all about the works of habitat enhancement. A timeline will need to be supplied of works which have already started through to completion works yet to be started.
    - Where the **work has not started**, details must be supplied of the type, size and condition of each proposed habitat on

[73] Regulation 8

the land and the projected performance as a result of those works.

- Where the **work has already commenced** details must be supplied of the type, size and condition of each proposed habitat on the land immediately before the commencement of works and the projected performance as a result of those works.

- If a **person other than a party to the section 106 agreement** or conservation covenant has the ability to enforce performance of any such habitat enhancement or maintenance works then their **details must be supplied**.

- **Details of the development** to which the relevant habitat enhancement works have been allocated must be supplied. In turn, the biodiversity value of the allocated habitat must be demonstrated as must the projected performance of the same.

- A **copy of the relevant section 106 agreement** or conservation covenant must be supplied.

- As ever, a **fee must be paid** and the details of that are set out below.

- **Allocation to a development.** Regulations permit the initial registration of a larger area of land followed by subsequent secondary registration of tranches of that initial registration block using different section 106 agreements or conservation covenants. This would allow the phasing of habitat production to meet developer-led demand over time. It also facilitates the habitat banking model.

  - However. there is a trade off for landowners who may not want to burden too much of their land with a section 106 agreement if they are unsure of the demand for Offsite Credits and hence the size of site that they will need.

  - The author has, to date, advised using a separate section 106 agreement for each area of land on which habitat will be created immediately or in the short term. This allows a risk based approach of not over committing land in an uncertain market. It permits allocation of that land to separate developments and complies with regulation 8 (f) of the Register Regulations which requires the end date of habitat creation or maintenance works to be identified.

  - That date will be the last day of the 30 year monitoring and enforcement period. By using a separate section 106 agreement for each area of habitat created then this end date can be identified at the outset.

- **Registry modification.**[74] Information regarding a registered piece of land may be modified by the relevant person. For example, if an area of 100 acres was initially registered but it transpires that only 10 acres was actually used for a particular development, then the record may be amended accordingly.

- **Registry removal.**[75] Land may be removed from the BNG Register either by the relevant person (e.g. if the land has not been used for the habitat improvement in question) or by Natural England (e.g. if the land is no longer eligible or was approved on the basis of false or misleading information).

- **Appeal.**[76] An appeal may be made against any decision made by Natural England with regards to application rejection,

[74] Regulation 12

[75] Regulation 24

[76] Regulation 30

amendments or removal of registered land. The appeal must be made to the First Tier Tribunal.

- **Use of Conservation Covenants.** Land can also be registered initially under a section 106 and later under a conservation covenant and vice versa. This seems to be aimed at permitting a later transition of agreements from section 106 to conservation covenants if desired.[77]

Conservation Covenants

The Act provides that habitat sites may be facilitated by the creation of conservation covenants. Conservation covenants, which came into force on 30 September 2022, are private agreements between landowners and responsible bodies which require the landowner to manage the land for conservation purposes. It is anticipated that responsible bodies are likely to be LPAs, charities, and organisations such as wildlife trusts.

Conservation covenants are seen as a key means of delivering BNG, as previously it was very difficult to bind successive owners and occupiers of land into long-term conservation agreements. Failure to deliver BNG can result in enforcement action under existing powers, as well as the new powers introduced in the Act by way of conservation covenants.

DEFRA published the criteria and application forms for becoming a responsible body on 27 July 2023.[78]

Unfortunately, conservation covenants have not been taken up with much enthusiasm, likely due to the perceived burden on responsible bodies of enforcing against landowners who are in breach of their BNG obligations.

---

77 Regulation 5 (4) and (5)

78 Conservation covenants: apply to become a responsible body – GOV.UK (www.gov.uk)

A Freedom of Information Act request made in late 2023[79] revealed that just 11 applications to be a responsible body had been received by DEFRA at that stage. There may, perhaps, be an opening of the floodgates following the publication of the aforementioned secondary legislation, but with applications having only increased to 15 as of January 2024 interest in such covenants seems to be limited for now.

Units[80]

As mentioned, the biodiversity of a site is calculated via the Biodiversity Metric with output measured in biodiversity units. The latest version of the Biodiversity Metric, published by DEFRA on 23 November 2023, supersedes version 4.0 previously published by Natural England.

A property's total biodiversity unit output is calculated by an assessor who meets the British Standard "process for designing and implementing biodiversity net gain" (BS 8683:2021) and, if needed, accredited in River Condition Assessment methodology.

The assessor collects data from the property, such as the type of habitats on the property and their distinguishing features (variety of plant/animal species, ecological conditions etc) and inputs the data into the Biodiversity Metric framework. The calculation is then reviewed by a third party, often a determining body or planning authority.

The Biodiversity Metric uses habitat features as an approximate measure for estimating the value of biodiversity net gain on a site. The metric takes into account the distance of the offsite BNG provision from the development site and will penalise the value of habitat creation accordingly. The greater the distance from the development, the lower the deemed value of the habitat. If a habitat bank is within the same LPA,

---

79 By the ever vigilant Julie Robinson of Roythornes

80 DEFRA Statutory Biodiversity Metric User Guide, Feb 2024 https://assets.publishing.service.gov.uk/media/65c60e0514b83c000ca715f3/The_Statutory_Biodiversity_Metric_-_User_Guide_.pdf

there is no penalty applied. If it is in the neighbouring LPA, then a 25% deduction is made. Beyond that, a 50% discount is applied. These deductions will increase the number of biodiversity credits required to satisfy the BNG objective.

Habitat banks operate on the same Biodiversity Metric framework. The resultant biodiversity units can then be transformed into Offsite Credits, which will be purchasable from habitat bank providers. Units can also be created by a developer in collaboration with a neighbouring landowner or within the development itself.

Risk multipliers and the advantage of habitat banks

The Biodiversity Metric accounts for the difficulty of creating or enhancing certain habitats through the use of "risk multiplier scores." There are three categories of risk multipliers:

- **Difficulty risk**, which represents the uncertainty in the effectiveness of the techniques used to create or enhance habitats from 0.67 for medium habitat and 0.33 for high and 0.1 for very high.

- **Spatial risk**, which as mentioned will apply a discount depending on the distance between the development site and the site from which biodiversity units are being acquired.

- **Temporal risk,** which represents the average time lag between the start of habitat creation or enhancement works and the target outcome. This is known as 'time to target condition' and is measured in years. The temporal risk multiplier (like all of the multipliers) is automatically applied by the Biodiversity Metric and changes depending on data input and will apply a penalty which varies from no penalty if it takes zero years down to a deduction of 0.32 if it takes 32 years to reach target condition.

- **Advanced or delayed action. A user** should adjust the temporal risk multiplier to account for any time difference between the loss and compensation.

    - The "**creation in advance**" function reflects the number of years habitat is created offsite in advance of clearance of the habitat on the development site (for example, when habitat banking is used).

    - The "**delay in starting habitat creation or enhancement**" function reflects the number of years the habitat is absent i.e. from clearance of the habitat on the development site to the start of habitat compensation (on or of site) for the loss.

  These functions should be applied for on-site and off-site delivery for all habitat types. They demonstrate how habitat banking can create habitats in advance of their being needed. Doing so takes advantage of the "creation in advance function" and avoids/mitigates the penalties of delay, difficulty of establishment and time to target.

Small Sites

Small sites are only required to achieve BNG from April 2024.

Small developments are defined as not major developments under the Town and Country Planning (Development Management Procedure) (England) Order 2015. This includes:

- Residential developments where the number of dwellings is between one and nine, or if this is unknown, the site area is less than 0.5 hectares

- Commercial developments where floor space created is less than 1,000 square metres or total site area is less than 1 hectare

- Developments that do not include the winning and working of minerals or the use of land for mineral-working deposits

- Developments that are not waste developments

If a project qualifies as a small site, developers can use either the standard statutory biodiversity metric tool or a simpler version of the tool called the small sites metric (SSM). The SSM cannot be used on sites where:

- habitats not available in the SSM are present;

- priority habitats are within the development site (excluding some hedgerows and arable field margins); or,

- European protected species are present on the development site.

Projects that make use of the SSM:

- **do not have to conduct a condition assessment** as part of its existing habitat survey, as the values are fixed for all assessed habitats.

- **do not need an ecologist**, as the tool permits site assessment by the developer or someone who is familiar with the site to conduct a survey. This could be the project manager, a gardener or a landscape architect. There is also a growing market of service providers offering automated net gain plans using the SSM.

<u>Local Nature Recovery Strategies</u>

The Biodiversity Metric also takes into account the strategic significance of certain sites. Local Nature Recovery Strategies (LNRS) will be implemented on a countrywide scale under the Act. These are seen as a way of reinforcing the existing duties of LPAs in promoting biodiversity in their local areas. LNRS are currently part of national policy and over time will be incorporated within local policies.

Areas designated as LNRS will be given priority for the purposes of offsetting. This means that there will be an advantage for landowners located within designated LNRS sites, and such sites will be given an increased weighting under the calculations in the metric.

Local nature recovery strategies identify the places and habitats that are most beneficial for nature; they will receive 15% more biodiversity units than if the same habitat were created elsewhere. The 15% figure is not absolute and will apply only if the site is formally identified in the local strategy. The bonus will be reduced to 10% if the location is ecologically desirable but not yet included within the local strategy.

Ecological corridors

Ecological corridors will also be considered as a possible advantage on the basis that ecological connectivity is an important concept in biodiversity. Landowners will therefore need to consider how their landholdings connect and also how they might work with other landowners in the area to provide a web of connected habitats, which may have a greater combined value than their individual parts.

Unit prices

- **Offsite Credits:**[81] Both the price and method of payment of Offsite Credits are negotiated between the seller and the buyer. Payment may be made as a lump sum, by instalments or by results. Government guidelines suggest the seller factor the costs of maintaining the land (e.g. monitoring and reporting, insurance, staff costs etc) into the final price. The value of an Offsite Credit is likely to be related to its distance from the development: the further away the source (e.g. the habitat bank selling the Offsite Credit) is from the site, the less valuable the unit. This is because of the operation of the Spatial Risk Multiplier (SRM) where if a habitat bank is within the same LPA,

81 https://www.gov.uk/guidance/sell-biodiversity-units-as-a-land-manager

then there is no penalty applied. If it is in the neighbouring LPA, then a 25% deduction is made in terms of the number of Offsite Credits generated by a site. Offsite Credits acquired further afield are discounted by 50%.[82] The actual effect on the market is difficult to judge at this stage as much will depend on demand and supply factors applying to each deal. However, if a developer has to buy more Offsite Credits the further afield they go then it seems reasonable that they will want to pay a lower unit price for those Offsite Credits than they might for a similar offering on their doorstep.

- **Statutory Credits:** Credit prices vary depending on the type of habitat being developed, ranging from £42,000 to £650,000 per credit.[83] As an option of last resort, statutory credits are intentionally priced uncompetitively to discourage their use. The credits themselves are also half the value of a biodiversity unit, meaning two credits must be purchased for every one unit that must be compensated for.[84]

What BNG means for landowners

- **A volatile market:** Drawing from the history of more mature environmental currencies such as carbon credits, BNG unit prices will likely be volatile as the newly-formed market seeks to find equilibrium. It also seems likely that there will initially be an oversupply of Offsite Credits when the England wide market is considered. However, there will be geographic mismatches where demand and supply do not equate. The market is looking very localised at the time of writing which is perhaps due to the

82 https://www.michelmores.com/agriculture-insight/biodiversity-net-gain-basics/

83 https://www.gov.uk/guidance/statutory-biodiversity-credit-prices

84 https://www.gov.uk/guidance/statutory-biodiversity-credit-prices

operation of the Spatial Risk Multipliers and the individual approaches of different LPAs.

What BNG means for LPAs

Local planning authorities (LPAs) can set policies to support BNG. They can identify local areas suitable for habitat creation and enhancement to help:

- landowners who want to sell Offsite Credits
- developers who need to comply with the BNG requirements

LPAs can make sure developers know about:

- the 10% BNG requirement
- local policy requirements for BNG, such as LNRS

If the LNRS has not yet been published, LPAs should say what plans are currently in place.

After the LPA grants planning permission for the development, the developer must then submit a biodiversity gain plan. The LPA will need to decide whether to approve the biodiversity gain plan by considering whether the 10% BNG is achieved. Developers cannot start work on a development and the LPA cannot publish a development on their register until the it has approved the biodiversity gain plan. This ensures that:

- onsite biodiversity gains that have been identified through the development's approved plans and drawings are appropriately secured;
- any Offsite Credits have been registered and allocated to the development; and

- Statutory Credits, if they are necessary, have been purchased.

BNG is not just a post-permission matter, however. To ensure the biodiversity gain objective is met and the condition can be discharged successfully, it is important that BNG is considered throughout the planning process. The National Planning Policy Framework emphasises that plans should identify and pursue opportunities for securing measurable net gains for biodiversity, and plans and decisions should minimise impacts and provide net gains for biodiversity.

Prior to the submission of a relevant planning application, applicants are encouraged to consider BNG early in the development process and factor it into site selection and design. Where appropriate, they should discuss BNG requirements for their development upfront with the relevant local planning authority utilising any pre-application advice services offered by them. This could help establish whether development proposals would be subject to BNG and, if they are, enable feedback on the proposed strategy for achieving the biodiversity gain objective as well as ensure consideration of the Biodiversity Gain Hierarchy to inform the design of the proposals.

When a planning application is submitted, there are minimum national information requirements related to BNG for those applications which, if planning permission was granted, would be subject to the general biodiversity gain condition. This will allow consideration of existing habitat baselines. Local planning authorities may also seek further information about the proposed strategy to meet the biodiversity gain objective for the development.

When determining a planning application, BNG will often be a material consideration. LPAs will want to consider, where relevant, whether the general biodiversity gain condition is capable of being discharged successfully through the imposition of conditions and agreements of section 106 planning obligations to secure significant onsite biodiversity gains and registered offsite biodiversity gains.

Finally, following the approval of the Biodiversity Gain Plan and commencement of development, LPAs will play an important role in monitoring the implementation of biodiversity net gain and, where appropriate, take enforcement action if conditions or obligations related to biodiversity net gain are not met.

LPAs as plan makers

Paragraph 179 of the National Planning Policy Framework states that to protect and enhance biodiversity and geodiversity, plans should among other things identify and pursue opportunities for securing measurable net gains for biodiversity. Planning authorities and neighbourhood planning bodies will therefore need to take account of the statutory framework for biodiversity net gain when preparing new policies in line with paragraph 179.

Plan-makers should highlight the statutory framework for BNG, but they do not need to include policies which duplicate the detailed provisions of this statutory framework. It will also generally be inappropriate for plans or supplementary planning documents to include policies or guidance which are inconsistent with this framework, for instance by applying BNG to exempt categories of development or encouraging the use of a different biodiversity metric or biodiversity gain hierarchy.

Plan-makers can complement the BNG statutory framework by including policies which support appropriate local offsite biodiversity sites for example. This includes whether specific allocated sites for development which contain biodiversity enhancements to support other developments meet their net gain objectives in line with LNRS.

Plan-makers may set a BNG objective above than the 10% minimum, either on an area-wide basis or for specific allocations for development. However, such policies will need to be evidenced, including as to local need for a higher percentage, local opportunities for a higher percentage and any impact on development viability. Consideration will also need to be given to how the policy will be implemented.

The BNG statutory framework involves the discharge of the general biodiversity gain condition following the grant of planning permission to ensure the objective that developments will meet the minimum requirement of at least 10% net gain. The determination of the Biodiversity Gain Plan under this condition is the mechanism to confirm whether the development meets the biodiversity gain objective. Development may not be begun until the Biodiversity Gain Plan is approved.

Given this, it would generally be inappropriate for decision makers, when determining a planning application for a development subject to biodiversity net gain, to refuse an application on the grounds that the biodiversity gain objective will not be met.

However, decision makers may need to consider more broadly whether the general condition is capable of being successfully discharged. Matters for consideration may include the following (but this is not an exhaustive list):

- the appropriate balance expected between onsite gains, off-site gains and the use of statutory biodiversity credits for the development, taking account of the biodiversity gain hierarchy

- whether the type and location of any significant onsite habitat enhancements proposed for onsite gains are appropriate, taking into account other policies to support biodiversity (including LNRS) and other wider objectives; and

- any planning conditions which need to be imposed to secure any significant onsite habitat enhancements, including any conditions requiring the maintenance of the enhancement for at least 30 years after the completion of the development.

Prior to the determination of the planning application, decision makers will also want to discuss with the applicant whether any section 106 planning obligations are required to secure either significant onsite habitat enhancements or offsite gains for the development.

For some planning applications (for instance, applications for outline planning permission where landscaping and layout are reserved matters), the implications for existing onsite habitats and the contribution to onsite gains may be uncertain at the time of the application's determination. In these cases, decision makers may want to consider what subsequent approvals will be necessary to ensure significant onsite habitat enhancements are appropriately secured.

<u>How do existing local policies apply following the introduction of mandatory biodiversity net gain?</u>

It would generally be inappropriate for decision makers to continue to give weight to aspects of existing local policies related to biodiversity gains which are inconsistent with the statutory framework for biodiversity net gain. The statutory provisions are an important material consideration that in many cases will take precedence over local planning policy. The statutory framework represents the appropriate national approach towards, and benchmark for, biodiversity gains in planning.

A local policy, for instance, which required a gain of at least 10% from new developments in anticipation of the statutory framework should no longer apply when determining applications for planning permission subject to biodiversity net gain, although it may continue to be a material consideration during a transition period and for other types of planning permission not yet subject to the statutory framework.

However, a policy which required a gain of greater than 10% on an area-wide basis or for an allocation may still be justified as the statutory biodiversity gain objective is for at least a 10% gain.

Decision makers should generally not give weight to local policy which requires biodiversity gains for types of development which would now be exempt under the statutory framework. Other local biodiversity policies which require specific enhancements to support biodiversity would continue to apply to these applications where appropriate.

Planning conditions are normally imposed on the grant of planning permission under section 70 (1) and section 72 of the Town and Country Planning Act 1990.

By contrast, the general biodiversity gain condition has a separate statutory basis as a planning condition under Paragraph 13 of Schedule 7A of the Town and Country Planning Act 1990. The condition is deemed to apply to every planning permission granted for the development of land in England (unless exemptions or transitional provisions apply), and there are separate provisions governing the Biodiversity Gain Plan.

To ensure applicants are clear about this distinction, the local planning authority must not include the general biodiversity gain condition in the list of conditions imposed in the written notice when granting planning permission.

Can a local planning authority apply planning conditions in relation to biodiversity net gain?

Local planning authorities have broad powers to impose planning conditions and can, where appropriate, include additional conditions relating to the delivery of biodiversity net gain.

A planning condition can be used to secure significant on-site habitat enhancements which are required to be secured and maintained for at least 30 years under paragraph 9 of Schedule 7A. Other potential conditions could include monitoring and reporting arrangements. Planning conditions should be appropriately worded to ensure effective compliance and enforcement of biodiversity net gain.

It is not appropriate to use planning conditions to secure funding for delivering or monitoring biodiversity net gain. These should be secured through section 106 planning obligations where justified.

Local planning authorities can agree to planning obligations (commonly referred to as section 106 agreements) to mitigate impacts of a development. This includes obligations relating to the delivery of significant on-site biodiversity enhancements, registered off-site biodiversity gains and the use of statutory credits.

Matters that could be covered in planning obligations include management and monitoring arrangements, dealing with excess net gains to be used for other developments, offsite gains and circumstances where credits can be used as a last resort. Where offsite gains are already registered and subject to a planning obligation or conservation covenant, it may not be necessary to tie them to development with another planning obligation.

Local planning authorities can charge a monitoring fee though section 106 planning obligations to cover the cost of monitoring and reporting on delivery of that section 106 agreement.

Planning obligations should be appropriately worded to ensure effective compliance and enforcement of biodiversity net gain.

Local planning authorities are encouraged to use and publish standard forms and templates to assist with the process of agreeing planning obligations to support biodiversity net gain. These could include model agreements and clauses (including those already published by other bodies), that could be made publicly available to help with the planning application process. Any further information required by the local planning authority, or issues raised by the applicant regarding planning obligations, should be addressed at an early stage of the planning application process.

Exemptions

The Exemptions regulations confirm that the BNG requirement will not apply to planning permissions made or granted before 1 April 2024 which relate to a small development as defined in the "small sites" section of this chapter.

The BNG requirement will also not apply to those planning permissions granted under section 73 of the Town and Country Planning Act 1990 where the original planning application was made before the commencement date of these regulations. This is where an application is made for permission to develop land which has already had planning permission given subject to conditions which have not been complied with.

A *de minimis* exception is also introduced where the development:

- does not impact a priority habitat; and
- impacts less than 25 square metres of habitat with biodiversity value greater than zero; and
- is less than 5 metres of linear habitat.

The BNG requirement will also not apply to householder applications, which means developments to an existing dwellinghouse or within its curtilage for any purpose incidental to its enjoyment. The definition does not extend to change of use applications or the alteration of the number of dwellings provided.

Any development linked to the HS2 project will not be caught by the BNG requirement and any Nationally Significant Infrastructure Projects will not be part of the BNG regime until November 2025.

Confirmation has been supplied that the BNG requirement will not apply if you need to obtain planning permission to create a biodiversity gain site for another development.

There is good news for the self-building community as well in that development of 9 or fewer dwellings will not be subject to these new BNG requirements providing the site is 0.5 hectares or less.

The Irreplaceable Habitats Regulations

These regulations define irreplaceable habitat which is essentially ancient trees and woodland, saltmarsh, blanket bog, lowland fens, limestone pavements and coastal sand dunes.

The effect of the regulations is to modify the BNG principles in terms of these important habitat types. There is no requirement to increase the biodiversity of such habitats by 10% and instead alternative arrangements must be made to minimise the effect of the development on the irreplaceable habitat. This requirement does not apply to phased development as Schedule 14 to the EA 2021 already provides for regulations to be drafted dealing with this scenario.

The Amendments Regulations

These regulations amend section 73 of the Town and Country Planning Act 1990 which deals with permission to develop land without complying with conditions previously attached.

The new regulations state that:

- If the section 73 conditions result in the same post-development biodiversity as specified in the original planning application, then the earlier biodiversity gain plan will be regarded as approved for the section 73 application.

- If the conditions affect the post-development biodiversity value of the onsite habitat as specified in the earlier biodiversity gain plan, then that previous plan will not be regarded as approved for the purpose of the permission granted under section 73.

- If the conditions attached to a section 73 permission do not change the effect of the development on onsite habitat which is irreplaceable habitat, a biodiversity gain plan previously approved as part of the original planning consent will suffice for the subsequent section 73 application.

The Fees Regulations

These regulations will come into force along with the Register Regulations and provide for a fine of £5,000 imposed by Natural England if false or misleading information is supplied to it. There will be a right to object to a fine imposition and a right of appeal if the process is completed. The fee schedule is as follows:

- The cost of **registering a site** on the BNG Register will be £639.
    - Each **subsequent allocation** of part or all of that land to a development will be £45.
- **Amending the BNG Register**
    - because of modifications made to a section 106 agreement or conservation covenant will cost £639.
    - because of incomplete or inaccurate information will cost £639.
    - An application to **remove an entry** will cost £89.
- **Removing an allocation** of habitat to a development will cost £45.

Marine Net Gain

Consultation

In June 2022, DEFRA opened a 12-week consultation to seek views regarding the definition and scope of introducing a marine net gain

(MNG) approach to infrastructure and development.[85] Broadly speaking, the principles of MNG are not dissimilar from those of the land-based BNG strategy by specifying a minimum threshold of overall biodiversity gain that must be achieved by new marine developments; developers must also adhere to a "mitigation hierarchy" in order to minimize any biodiversity loss.[86] Compliance will also be assessed via a three-step assessment framework process similar to BNG:

1. Use the assessment framework to measure the environmental impact of a project.

2. Outline the benefits of proposed interventions to offset the impact quantified in step 1.

3. Demonstrate that the proposed interventions will surpass the minimum net gain threshold.

DEFRA sought respondents' views on three major elements of MNG strategy: its definition, its scope and what consists of improving marine biodiversity.

MNG Definition

- **MNG will measure impacts on habitats and species.** DEFRA contrasted MNG with BNG by highlighting the "dynamic nature of the marine environment;" MNG projects may therefore need to take into account the impact of a development on mobile species.

---

85 https://naturalengland.blog.gov.uk/2022/06/07/marine-net-gain-leaving-the-marine-environment-in-better-state/

86 https://consult.defra.gov.uk/defra-net-gain-consultation-team/consultation-on-the-principles-of-marine-net-gain/supporting_documents/Consultation%20on%20the%20Principles%20of%20Marine%20Net%20Gain.pdf

- **MNG will seek to incorporate environmental benefits underpinned by biodiversity.** As outlined previously, MNG should seek to implement broader net gain principles in its implementation.

- **MNG will take a "nature first" approach whilst recognizing wider environmental benefits.** While non-biodiversity impact will be factored in when calculating MNG, they will be second-order considerations. MNG should not be "a tool to pursue wider environmental objectives as an alternative to biodiversity objectives."

- **MNG assessments will not include potentially positive incidental impacts whose benefits are subject to significant uncertainty.** Projects of uncertain or unproven benefit will not be included in the scope of the policy.

- **MNG requirements will be proportionate and appropriate to the scale and type of development.** This will require development of "an objective and consistent means of measuring the main development's impacts," including residual impacts.

MNG Scope

- **MNG will be a mandatory requirement applicable to all marine development**, subject to minimal thresholds and other exemptions. In this, MNG would be similar to mandatory BNG under the Environment Act 2021.

- **MNG enforcement will be underpinned by a composite of legislation**, including the Marine and Coastal Access Act 2009, the Planning Act 2008 and the Petroleum Act 1998.

- **MNG will be restricted to economic activities that can be considered development**, e.g. construction and infrastructure installation. Decommissioning, maintenance etc would likely be precluded.

What constitutes meaningful impact

- **MNG will incentivise measures to both improve habitats and/or alleviate pressures on marine ecosystems.** An example of improvement projects would be species reintroduction, while pressure alleviation would include reducing fishing activity etc.

- **DEFRA will be open to exploring novel marine conservation measures.** While novel techniques must have evidentiary backing, DEFRA stresses that MNG is an opportunity to encourage innovation, particularly given the relative immaturity of fields such as subtidal habitat restoration.

Responses

In March 2023, DEFRA released a summary of the responses it received from the public.[87] Broadly speaking, respondents were in favour of the proposals outlined by the department, however there was call for greater clarity on certain subjects. For example, when discussing measuring the impact of projects, respondents emphasized the need to consider cumulative impacts of both developments and external pressures rather than thinking on individual impacts in isolation. For example, when considering a reduction in species diversity, it is important to recognize externalities beyond the control of individual projects, e.g. species disappearing due to wider climate change.

Several respondents suggested expanding MNG scope to include terrestrial developments that could impact the marine environment, such as fisheries, ports and shipping. Respondents also emphasized the need to adhere to the "polluter pays" principle to ensure that the party

87 https://www.gov.uk/government/consultations/consultation-on-the-principles-of-marine-net-gain/outcome/summary-of-responses

responsible for producing pollution be the one to pay for the damage caused by said pollution. In that, MNG should not be used to alleviate the pressures of other industries.

CHAPTER FOUR

NUTRIENT NEUTRALITY

What is Nutrient Neutrality?

Changes to the nutrient levels in our soil and water can cause a domino effect with dramatic consequences for the environment. Excess phosphorous and nitrogen levels in waterways contribute to the growth of algal blooms, leading to eutrophication, which causes oxygen levels for fish and other aquatic life to be reduced significantly. The chief sources of these excess nutrients include wastewater treatment and agricultural pollution.[88]

Nutrient neutrality is the process of ensuring that a project or development does not result in higher phosphate and nitrate levels for vulnerable watercourses within a catchment area. Under the Conservation of Habitats and Species Regulations 2017[89] ("**Habitats Regulations**"), local planning authorities must make an "appropriate assessment" of the ecological impact of new developments within designated habitat sites.

In 2018, The European Court of Justice ruled on the landmark "Dutch N" case[90]. The case informs the way in which relevant legislation is applied to pollution-related matters, in particular, nitrogen and

---

88 https://www.gov.uk/government/publications/nutrient-pollution-reducing-the-impact-on-protected-sites/nutrient-pollution-reducing-the-impact-on-protected-sites

89 https://www.legislation.gov.uk/uksi/2017/1012/contents/made

90 *Coöperatie Mobilisation for the Environment and Vereniging Leefmilieu v College van gedeputeerde staten Van Limberg* [2019] Env LR 27

phosphorus, and the limits placed on their runoff to stop them from polluting the wider environment. The relevant legislation is contained in Articles 6(2) and 6(3) of the EU Habitats Directive (92/43/EEC), as implemented by the Habitats Regulations.

Part of the driver behind the EU Habitats Directive was to improve the conservation status of natural habitats and species designated for protection. Areas are designated as in an "unfavourable condition," and the overall conservation goal is to improve the site to a "favourable condition" designation. Each Special Area of Conservation (SACs), Special Protection Area (SPAs) and Ramsar Sites (i.e., wetlands of international importance) has its own set of conservation objectives.[91] Nutrient neutrality mitigation is meant to be a temporary measure: sites should be improving their nutrient balance to the point where no mitigation should be required at all.[92]

This book will use the shorthand of **Habitat Sites** to describe these protected waterways which are the focus of nutrient neutrality. The location of the land being used for mitigation measures whether that be cessation of farming or wetland construction will be defined as the **Mitigation Site**.

Habitat Regulations Assessment

All projects and proposals affecting a Habitat Site (established or proposed), as well as areas secured as sites compensating for damage done

[91] https://designatedsites.naturalengland.org.uk/SiteSearch.aspx

[92] **Natural England, Nutrient Neutrality and Mitigation: A summary guide and frequently asked questions** (NE776) ("**Summary Guide**") at p.4 (last updated February 2024): *This approach is not mandatory and, if they prefer, competent authorities can determine their own solutions as appropriate. Nutrient neutrality is intended to be an interim solution whilst we return Habitats Sites to favourable condition.*

to Habitat Sites[93] must first pass a Habitats Regulations Assessment (**HRA**) conducted by a competent authority, such as a planning inspector or a licensing public body.[94] There are up to three stages to an HRA:

1. **Screening**, where the proposal is assessed to determine whether it will have a significant effect on the site's conservation objectives. If no significant effect is found, the HRA ends and no further steps are needed.

2. **Appropriate assessment**, where the authority decides there is a risk of significant effect and a more detailed and thorough assessment is required. This will include a thorough analysis of the site's integrity and what if any mitigation measures can be implemented.

3. **Derogation.** Competent authorities have a limited power to allow a proposal that has failed the integrity assessment to proceed regardless. There are three legal tests to determine whether a proposal qualifies as derogation:

    a. There are **no feasible alternative solutions** that would be less damaging or avoid damage to the site;

    b. The proposal must be carried out for **imperative reasons of overriding public interest;** and

    c. The **necessary compensatory measures** can be secured.

As a result of the Habitats Regulations, LPAs now require an HRA for proposed changes in land use or development in the catchment areas of Habitat Sites. This is to ascertain whether there will be any adverse effects

---

[93] SACs, SPAs. Ramsar sites are given like effect by way of government policy – see para 187 of the National Planning Policy Framework (revised 19.12.23)

[94] https://www.gov.uk/guidance/habitats-regulations-assessments-protecting-a-european-site

due to the project's location, size or nature. Mitigation solutions are required where adverse effects have been found. The areas in question are detailed in the next section of this chapter.

An HRA will be required for any relevant development as part of the planning process. This requirement does not only apply at outline stage, but continues until the local planning authority had made the "implementing decision". As such, the relevant LPA will require an HRA:

- at outline stage;
- at reserved matters stage if no HRA was undertaken at outline stage;
- at reserved matters stage even if a HRA was undertaken at outline stage if there has been a material change in circumstances; and
- when discharging conditions on full or outline permissions, whether or not the conditions relate specifically to nutrients.

Screening

Competent authorities such as LPAs must[95] make an appropriate assessment of the implications of such plans or projects in view of the conservation objectives of the protected site before these can go ahead. The initial screening is a simple assessment to determine whether the proposal is:

a. likely to have a significant effect on certain protected sites, either alone or in combination with other plans or projects, and

b. directly connected with or necessary to the management of the protected site.

---

95 See regulation 63 of the Habitats Regulations.

The authority will consider the proposal's integral design features or characteristics such as its layout, timing and location. If there is no risk to the site, then the HRA is concluded. Otherwise, the authority proceeds to the next step.

Appropriate assessment

The 'Appropriate Assessment' (**AA**) stage of the HRA must be carried out before an LPA will grant planning permission. This assessment includes determining whether adverse effects on site integrity can be ruled out (the 'integrity test'). At this stage Natural England (**NE**) must be consulted and measures to mitigate the impact can be considered and put forward (such as nutrient neutrality) to try to rule out such adverse effects. NE will need to be satisfied that the mitigation measures proposed will achieve nutrient neutrality.

NE advises that the LPA must have practical certainty that the nutrient neutrality measures relied on in an AA will be implemented and in place at the relevant time, e.g. secured and funded for the lifetime of the development's effects. In addition, all HRAs must be undertaken in consultation with NE.

NE have published a document entitled "Nutrient Neutrality Principles"[96] which sets out the approach which must be taken to ensure that any mitigation project will meet the requirements of the Habitats Regulations.

NE's advice is that any nutrient neutrality measures relied on in an AA should:

- Ensure that no reasonable scientific doubt remains as to the absence of effects of nitrogen and phosphorous pollution;

---

96 D2022 00135724 TIN186 – Nutrient Neutrality Principles [FINAL]-V2PL (1).pdf

- Be adequately secured through legally binding commitments and funded so that they are in place for perpetuity – defined by NE as 80-125 years;

- Be preventative in nature both temporally and spatially:

  - Temporally:

    - Consideration will need to be given as to (i) when the mitigation measures will come online and (ii) when the pollutants will enter the Habitats Site – an obvious example being phased development;

    - There may be a time lag between the effects of the development impacting the Habitats Site and the benefits of the nutrient mitigation scheme being felt at the Habitats Site;

  - Spatially:

    - If the development is within the boundary of the Habitat Site then the Mitigation Site will need to be upstream of where the development wastewater will enter the Habitat Site;

    - If the development is outside of the boundary of the Habitat Site (but within its catchment area) then the Mitigation Site can be upstream or downstream of the development as long as it provides the offsetting before impacting the Habitat Site

- Not to undermine the objective of restoring the Habitat Site to favourable condition;

- Not to double count measures that are already in place or must be put in place to protect, conserve or restore the Habitat Site to allow development to proceed;

- Be carefully justified and calculated so that the precautionary principle is adhered to; and

- Ensure that there is no real risk that the existing land use at the development site or Mitigation Site undermines the conservation objective to restore the Habitat Site to a favourable condition.

Previously consented as well as existing schemes fall within this requirement. This includes LPAs discharging planning conditions, approving reserved matters or granting minor amendments to existing planning consents.

Hurdles to approval

With regards to the temporal prevention requirement, the author has experienced issues in recent projects completed on behalf of clients. For instance, NE have asked for a hydrogeological assessment of the Mitigation Site late in the stages of the project. This is because the water takes a considerable time to flow from the Mitigation Site to the Habitats Site, meaning that the houses could be occupied before the water (newly stripped of its phosphorous and nitrogen through the mitigation measures) finds its way through the soil strata to the Habitats Site. In those circumstances, once the transit time for the waterflow to the Habitats Site has been calculated, authorities will not permit the occupation of the dwellings until that time period has elapsed.

LPAs have embargoed granting planning consents or discharging conditions until clear HRA assessments or solutions have been put in place and proven to work. The embargoes have created delays and additional expenses to residential development in affected LPA areas. The Housebuilders Federation ("**HBF**") estimates that 50-60k new homes are currently held up. HBF also estimates that the cost of mitigating phosphate, for example, is around £5,000 per consented dwelling.

Natural England Guidance

In its role as statutory consultee, NE may advise on the scope of mitigation required. LPAs must have regard to any representations made by NE in this capacity.[97]

When the initial advice was first issued back in 2019, NE focused on areas in the south and west of England. The advice concerned development within the catchment areas of Habitat Sites with an aim to achieve nutrient neutrality.

The key areas targeted by NE (amongst others) include:

- Cornwall – the Camel estuary;
- Essex – the Orwell and the Stour;
- Kent – the Great Stour;
- Hampshire and Dorset – the Solent;
- Herefordshire – the Wye and the Lugg;
- Shropshire – the Clun;
- Somerset – the Levels;
- Suffolk – the Deben estuary; and
- Wiltshire – the Avon.

[97] Regulation 63(3) Habitats Regulations

Coastal and marine areas such as the Solent suffer from an excess of nitrates, whereas for inland freshwater environments such as the Somerset Levels it is phosphates that are of concern.

Revised Guidance

In 2020 and again in 2022,[98] NE issued advice to LPAs and others on the assessment of new plans and projects under Regulation 63 of the Habitats Regulations. The 2022 Guidance clarified which protected sites were considered to be in unfavourable condition (i.e. unfavourable conservation status)[99] and that:

> *Where the plan or project will (or it cannot be ascertained that it will not) contribute additional significant nutrients, alone or in-combination directly to, or upstream of, any unfavourable location which is important for maintaining or restoring the sensitive designated interest features, then Natural England advises that either there is a Likely Significant Effect (LSE) or a LSE cannot be ruled out and therefore, an Appropriate Assessment should be undertaken.*[100]

A development will have the potential to impact a water-dependent protected site where there is hydrological connectivity between the two.[101] Logically, where there is hydrological connectivity which could cause adverse effects, there is also the potential to take steps to avoid or reduce such effects.

---

98 *Water Quality and Nutrient Neutrality Advice* (NE785) (**2022 Guidance**)

https://publications.naturalengland.org.uk/file/5133936477601792 Last issued on 16/03/22. Among other things, this enclosed NE's **Summary Guide** and NE's **Principles** documents referred to below.

99 2022 Guidance, Annex C at p.12-15

100 2022 Guidance, Annex A, Section 2.0 at p.8

101 2022 Guidance at p.3

NE also set out[102] the various situations where nutrient neutrality may not be an appropriate mitigation measure, and identifies in each case the potential geospatial constraints that could apply (e.g. those cases where mitigation would need to be in the exact same location as the impact, or within the same part of the groundwater catchment, or in limited areas upstream of the development).

NE's *Nutrient Neutrality and Nutrient Mitigation summary guide and frequently asked questions* document (**NE's Summary Guide**), which was enclosed with the 2022 Guidance, states:

> *Where developments would fail[103] the requirements of the Habitats Regulations appropriate assessment, developers may be asked to take action to mitigate impacts through nutrient neutrality such as:*
>
> - *building additional mitigation into their plans onsite;*
> - *working with the LPA to arrange for mitigation offsite; and*
> - *purchasing nutrient credits via a nutrient trading scheme (where other landowners in the catchment have taken action to reduce their nutrient load) or buying credits through the Natural England-led Nutrient Mitigation Scheme*[104] (emphasis added).

[102] 2022 Guidance, Annex C at p.15-16

[103] In some situations, an LPA's conclusion could be that the development should not go ahead because there are insufficient mitigation options available. An LPA could then decide to consider whether to begin the derogation process to enable the development to go ahead, despite the adverse impact.

[104] https://publications.naturalengland.org.uk/publication/6248597523005440 Summary Guide at p.5

NE's guidance is not legally binding.[105] However, as explained earlier, LPAs must have regard to any representations made by NE in its role as a statutory consultee under the Habitats Regulations.

The 2022 Guidance[106] added a further 42 LPAs in addition to the existing 32 bringing the total number affected to 74. Previously unaffected LPAs in areas such as Cumbria, Northumberland, Cheshire and parts of Yorkshire, for example, will now have to implement mitigation plans for new developments.

This area spans 27 catchments under the supervision (wholly or in part) of 74 local planning authorities. NE advised that "projects and plans may only go ahead at these sites if the increase in wastewater that is produced by the assumed population increases, from developments, will not cause additional nutrient pollution."[107]

Each LPA employs their own discretion to ensure that developments do not cause additional nutrient pollution; however, a Court of Appeal ruling held that adherence to the 2022 Guidance is sufficient to ensure that the LPA is compliant with the requirements confirmed by the Dutch N case.[108]

---

105 See Sir Keith Lindblom sitting in the Court of Appeal in R (Wyatt) v Fareham Borough Council [2022] EWCA Civ 983 at para 56 in relation to NE's 2020 guidance but in our view, the same could be said of the 2022 Guidance: *It is an advisory document, which is neither mandatory in effect nor prescriptive of a single correct procedure to be followed. It contains guidance, whose purpose is to assist competent authorities in performing their functions under the habitats legislation.*

106 NE785 Revised Edition Natural England Water Quality and Nutrient Neutrality Advice (16 March 2022).pdf

107 https://www.gov.uk/government/publications/nutrient-pollution-reducing-the-impact-on-protected-sites/nutrient-pollution-reducing-the-impact-on-protected-sites

108 R (Wyatt) v Fareham Borough Council & Natural England [2022] EWCA Civ 983

NE provided an updated national map showing the affected catchments. As a result, some existing areas have been assigned new catchments, that now need to be nutrient neutral. The new advice includes a 'National Generic Nutrient Neutrality Methodology'[109] along with specific catchment calculators and an updated catchment map showing the 27 new catchment areas.[110]

The 2022 Guidance now also includes several areas in the Midlands and the North. Developers in these catchments will need to demonstrate nutrient neutrality before planning permission can be granted. Not only will a developer have to establish to the LPA's satisfaction that mitigation is sufficient and nutrient neutrality is secured (either on-site or off), but NE will also need to sign-off. As part of the appropriate assessment stage of the HRA, there is a statutory 21-day consultation with NE.

The four-stage process for determining a nutrient budget remains largely the same. However, the new generic methodology introduces the following new variables at stages two and three of the methodology in relation to leaching rates:

- operational catchment;
- soil drainage type;
- average annual rainfall; and
- whether the site is within a Nitrate Vulnerable Zone (NVZ).

These new variables impact hugely on the leachate kg/ha of nitrate and phosphate for each of the individual land use types. Therefore, the land

109 NECR459 Edition 1 Nutrient Neutrality Generic Methodology.pdf

110 https://www.local.gov.uk/pas/topics/environment/nutrient-neutrality-and-planning-system

use nutrient export coefficient for both existing and future land use differs from the previous methodology calculations.

The Government's Planning Advisory Service has confirmed that these updated tools will change some of the figures used in nutrient budgets and developers will need to rerun their calculations using the new relevant calculators.

Types of development

All changes to land use or development that might cause additional nutrient loading are subject to nutrient neutrality requirements. This has a clear implication for improvements carried out on agricultural holdings: if farmers are planning on increasing livestock numbers, then new developments such as livestock sheds and slurry stores will have to satisfy the nutrient neutrality requirements of the HRA as set out below. Poultry farmers have to deal with the impact of both nutrient run off and the problem of ammonia emissions for their broiler or laying sheds. This latter air quality issue requires the installation of air scrubbers to combat the problem.

Calculating the nutrient burden

The generic methodology produced by NE involves a four-stage process for determining a nutrient budget for a given development; this takes into account the operational catchment, soil drainage type, average annual rainfall and whether the site is within a Nitrate Vulnerable Zone (NVZ):

1. Calculate the proposed development's total nitrogen/phosphate that would be discharged into the catchment (A);

2. Calculate existing (pre-development) nitrogen/phosphate from the current land use of the development site (B);

3. Calculate nitrogen/phosphate for the non-built land uses proposed for the development site, such as public open space (C);

4. Calculate the change in total nitrogen/phosphate due to the development: (A – B +/- C) including the 20% precautionary buffer.

If the result of Stage 4 is positive, then mitigation is required. If it is negative, mitigation is not required.

Each LPA has been provided with catchment-specific calculators to support a consistent approach to the assessment of nutrient neutrality across all affected catchments in England.

Example Calculation

The following is an example of a nutrient neutrality calculation for the Poole Harbour Rivers Catchment which has issues with both Phosphorous and Nitrogen run off.

The example assumes a development of 1,000 dwellings and the first page of the spreadsheet calculates the nutrient impact on the Habitat Site by inputting assumptions as to occupancy (2.4 people per house) and water usage of 120 litres per day.

The development will drain to the Blackheath Wastewater Treatment Works (WwTW) which is currently licensed to emit 8mg of Phosphorous per litre and 27mg of Nitrogen. These permit limits vary and the higher they are the less mitigation will be needed and vice versa. The permit levels are determined based on statutory water quality standards and objectives.

It can be seen in the table below that the permit levels post 2030 are much lower than the current requirements. This is because The Levelling Up and Regeneration Act 2023[111] has included provisions which will see the onus to tackle nutrient neutrality problems switched from developers to the water companies. They will be required to upgrade wastewater

[111] Section 168

treatment works, which discharge into the protected watercourses, to ensure that effluent is within acceptable limits (being not more than 10mg/l for nitrogen and 0.25mg/l for phosphorus).

All nutrient neutrality calculations are required[112] to assume that these improvement works will happen and so a pre and post 2030 figure is given in the calculator. As can be seen from the example below, the post 2030 figure is considerably lower in terms of the mitigation requirements with phosphorous dropping from 841.54 to 23.67 kg and nitrogen from 2840.18 to 946.73 kg.

Water infrastructure information		
Description of required information	**Data entry column**	**Additional data entry column**
Date of first occupancy (dd/mm/yyyy):		
Average occupancy rate (people/dwelling or people/unit):	2.40	
Water usage (litres/person/day):	120	
Development Proposal (dwellings/units):	1000	
Wastewater treatment works:	Blackheath WwTW	
Current wastewater treatment works P permit (mg TP/litre):	**8**	
Current wastewater treatment works N permit (mg TN/litre):	**27**	
Post 2030 WwTW P permit (mg TP/litre):	**0.25**	
Post 2030 WwTW N permit (mg TN/litre):	**10**	
Final calculation of nutrient load from wastewater		
Description of values generated	**Values generated**	
Post-2030 Stage 1 Nutrient Loading		
Additional population (people):	**2400**	
Wastewater by development (litres/day):	**288000**	
Annual wastewater TP load (kg TP/yr):	**23.67**	
Annual wastewater TN load (kg TN/yr):	**946.73**	
Pre-2030 Stage 1 Nutrient Loading		
Annual wastewater TP load (kg TP/yr):	**841.54**	
Annual wastewater TN load (kg TN/yr):	**2840.18**	

The next stage of the calculation is to insert the catchment area details, soil drainage type, annual rainfall and whether the Mitigation Site is located within a Nitrate Vulnerable Zone (NVZ). The existing use of the

112 Schedule 15 amending Part 6 of the Conservation of Habitats and Species Regulations 2017

Mitigation Site is also entered – pig farming in this example.

Current land use information				
Description of required information	**Data entry Column**			
Operational Catchment:	Poole Harbour Rivers			
Soil drainage type:	Slightly impeded drainage			
Annual average rainfall (mm):	750.1 - 800			
Within Nitrate Vulnerable Zone (NVZ):	Yes			
Current land uses				
Existing land use type(s)	**Area (ha)**	**Annual phosphorus nutrient export (kg TP/yr)**	**Annual nitrogen nutrient export (kg TN/yr)**	**Notes on data**
Pig	100.00	**53.60**	**4343.92**	
Totals:	100	**53.60**	**4343.92**	

The use of the Mitigation Site for pig farming produces a phosphorous export of 53.6 kg and nitrogen of 4343.92 kg per year.

That is then contrasted with the future use of the Mitigation Site (Greenspace in this example) which produces phosphorous and nitrogen exports or 2kg and 300kg respectively.

Future land uses			
New land use type(s)	**Area (ha)**	**Annual phosphorus nutrient export (kg TP/yr)**	**Annual nitrogen nutrient export (kg TN/yr)**
Greenspace	100.00	**2.00**	**300.00**
Totals:	**100**	**2.00**	**300.00**

These land use change figures are then subtracted from each other to give mitigation budget figures of 51.6 kg of phosphorous and 4043.92 kg of nitrogen.

Total nutrient budget calculations	
Description of values generated	**Values generated**
Wastewater TP load (kg TP/year):	23.67
Net land use TP change (kg TP/year):	-51.60
P budget (kg TP/year):	-27.93
P budget + 20% buffer (kg TP/year):	-27.93
Wastewater TN load (kg TN/year):	946.73
Net land use TN change (kg TN/year):	-4043.92
TN budget:	-3097.19
TN budget + 20% buffer:	-3097.19
Annual Nutrient Budget	
The total annual phosphorus load to mitigate is (kg TP/yr):	0.00
The total annual nitrogen load to mitigate is (kg TN/yr):	0.00
Pre-2030 Nutrient Budget	
The total annual phosphorus load to mitigate is (kg TP/yr):	947.93
The total annual nitrogen load to mitigate is (kg TN/yr):	0.00

When these land use change figures are applied to the wastewater nutrient loads there is a pre-2030 requirement for 947.93 kg of phosphorus but no nitrogen requirement. Post 2030, there is no mitigation requirement at all and 27.93 kg of phosphorus credits would be available to sell in the marketplace.

This disparity caused by the 2030 threshold is creating a new and alternative market for short-term nature-based solutions to bridge the mitigation gap until 2030. Many farmers and landowners would be far more willing to cease agricultural production for a six-year period and supply nutrient credits to a developer who might have another source of credits for the post 2030 period.

On-site options

It is possible to achieve nutrient neutrality on-site via the creation of large-scale wetlands, woodlands and fallow habitats. In practice, however, this is unlikely unless there is a significant open space provision within the development boundary, as neutrality measures are often very onerous and land hungry. Solutions also need to work in perpetuity (or at least for as long as the development is required), which can be a heavy burden on developers. Packaged private water treatment plants are one solution, but these require material investment in front-end infrastructure before other development can take place.

Off-site options

Off-site options are emerging as popular alternative mitigation solutions. One approach is to purchase nutrient 'credits': third-party landowners take agricultural land out of production and change the land use to woodland, heathland, saltmarsh, wetland, or conservation grassland to generate credits. For example, agricultural land used for poultry has a nitrogen leaching rate of 70.7 kgN/ha/yr, whereas woodland has a leaching rate of 5 kgN/ha/yr, creating a healthy nutrient deficit, which can be used to offset the effects of development.

NE advises that mitigation land is maintained for a minimum of 80-125 years. This significant obligation means that many developers may wish to buy credits from third-party landowners in a one-time transaction, allowing the developers to move on without the need to maintain the habitat themselves.

Many landowners are exploring the ability to benefit from several positive environmental outcomes on the same piece of land. This may include the receipt of both public money in the form of the new Environmental Land Management Scheme (ELMS), as well as private funds, such as those arising from nutrient neutrality. This opportunity is known as "stacking" and is detailed in Chapter 1.

Unlike the new mandatory biodiversity net gain requirement, NE has called for mitigation sites to be provided within the same local catchment area as the development. This greatly reduces the potential to find off-site land which can deliver solutions at a viable cost.

LPAs are considering (and in some cases are already implementing) credit schemes of their own. For example, Havant Borough Council developed its own nutrient neutrality scheme in which the proceeds of the credits go towards the creation of large-scale wetlands, woodlands and meadows to mitigate against the effect of development.

The market value of these credits can fluctuate wildly between different catchment areas as each area has their own levels of supply and demand. This demand/supply mismatch includes types of nutrients: in some areas, nitrates are the main problem, whereas in others, phosphates are the issue.

Securing land use change

Conservation covenants were introduced in the Act and came into force on 30 September 2022. These are private agreements between landowners and "responsible bodies" such as wildlife trusts. The agreements can be used to enforce future management of mitigation land by creating positive obligations which automatically bind successors in title. This accords with NE's view that offsite mitigation land should ideally be maintained in perpetuity.

What does this mean for developers?

Nutrient neutrality can dramatically impact development plans. As such:

- Developers must carry out sufficient due diligence and take technical advice as regards the impact of being in a "nutrient neutral area" or the likelihood of being in such an area.

- Developers may be more likely to seek to link agreed minimum prices to net developable acres rather than gross acres so as exclude land required for mitigation measures.

- Developers may seek to increase the land they control to accommodate mitigation measures.

- Developers may seek additional rights over further land held by the seller.

- Where developers are already collaborating on larger sites, consideration will need to be given to the developing planning picture.

These new regulations could also change developer land acquisition strategies, prompting developers to move away from unconditional acquisitions of land with the benefit of outline planning consent to acquisitions conditional on detailed consent or reserved matters approval on the basis of an acceptable HRA and mitigation measures.

In summary, all developers and landowners, with interests in projects or land in affected areas, should reconsider their legal and commercial positions. Prompt action may be necessary and collaboration with landowners and others will be vital in finding the most effective solutions.

Nutrient Mitigation Scheme

The nutrient neutrality scheme as outlined until this point relies on private deals struck between developers and landowners. While flexible, this does carry with it an element of price volatility and issues of supply and demand. The Nutrient Mitigation Scheme ("**NMS**") is a new effort by the Government to provide a standardized method for developers to offset nutrient pollution. In 2022, the Secretary of State directed NE to operate "strategic mitigation schemes" to tackle nutrient pollution within relevant catchments. [113] Such schemes "allow developers the opportunity to purchase the benefit of off-site mitigation works from NE in order to provide information to local planning authorities to show that, in their

[113] https://www.gov.uk/government/publications/natural-englands-nutrient-mitigation-scheme-for-developers/how-to-apply-for-nutrient-mitigation-credits-from-natural-england

and NE's opinion, the proposed development has addressed nutrient pollution issues under the Habitats Regulations."[114]

As explained in NE's Summary Guide:

> *"The Government wants to support the delivery of sustainable development, and so we are providing up to £30 million to speed up the delivery of nature-based solutions from which developers can purchase nutrient credits, allowing them to discharge their planning conditions."*

The NMS was launched in on 31 March 2023 in response to this Government direction. The scheme is in its pilot stage: it is currently limited to the Tees Catchment and is meant to be rolled out in other catchments as is develops. Feasibility studies are being conducted in a further five catchments to identify the next tranche of mitigation sites and landowners will be invited to offer land as potential sites for nutrient mitigation.

The scheme, initially funded by DEFRA, establishes wetlands and woodlands which will lead to the creation of Nutrient Mitigation Scheme Credits ("**NMS Credits**") accredited by NE. Such accreditation will presumably follow the same guidance and calculations already published by NE and being used to validate nutrient credits from private schemes. The architecture of these schemes is similar to other credit systems: developers purchase nutrient credits to offset the environmental costs of new developments.

The Government has made it clear that such private arrangements can continue and will exist alongside the NMS. As with other environmental schemes, the Government's emphasis is on working together with, not crowd out the private sector. Private schemes are likely to fulfil an

[114] https://www.gov.uk/government/publications/nutrient-pollution-direction-to-natural-england-on-strategic-mitigation-schemes/nutrient-pollution-direction-to-natural-england-on-strategic-mitigation-schemes

important role in providing nutrient credits as the NMS is established and thereafter so as to ensure a competitive marketplace. That said, the increased supply of credits from the NMS is having a direct effect on the price of private market nutrient credits.

To date, the NMS Credit price has been set by reference to the cost of providing the underlying mitigation scheme. The NMS Tees catchment area pilot is limited to nitrogen; it remains to be seen what price will be set for phosphorus credits when the NMS is extended to other catchment areas in due course. If it follows the nitrogen NMS credit framework, there should not be any reason why phosphorus NMS credits would be materially more expensive. However, this is not the position in the private marketplace where the forces of supply and demand have driven the price of phosphorus credits far above those of nitrogen.

Options for developers: go private now or wait for NMS to become more established?

So where does this leave a developer with an urgent requirement for nutrient credits to progress a planning application? The answer is perhaps to continue with the private deal currently being negotiated. There is the obvious choice of waiting to see if NMS Credits are cheaper, but that may not be an option in urgent cases or considered too much of a risk given the economic headwinds already blowing.

It is worth noting that section 101(4) of the Act makes it clear that statutory credits for biodiversity net gain must be priced at such a level so that the registration of land in the biodiversity gain sites register is not discouraged. As this registration is the only way to create a private market for credits, the price of statutory credits will inevitably need to be higher than their private equivalent.

It remains to be seen whether NMS Credits come with a similar price control mechanism but there is no sign of one at the time of writing. Regardless, developers are likely to benefit from the greater competition in the market, which will result from the increased availability of mitigation options whether they be public or private in nature.

The NMS was given a boost in the Chancellor's 2023 Autumn Statement[115] with £110 million of funding provided to the Local Nutrient Mitigation Fund to allow LPAs to bring forward innovative mitigation schemes.

This highlights the fact that there are numerous ways to provide mitigation for nutrient run off:

- Creation or restoration of new semi-natural habitats such as woodlands and wetlands;
- Treatment wetlands to remove nutrients;
- Use of Sustainable Urban Drainage Systems (SUDs) into existing developments;
- Replacing inefficient septic tanks with Package Treatment Plants;
- Provision of new WwTW facilities managed by an OFWAT appointed statutory sewage undertaker; and
- Short term agricultural management such as fallowing land and provision of buffer strips.

Nutrient Mitigation Scheme Credits

One unit is equivalent to one kilogram of nitrogen and the units are sold by NE in rounds, with the price set before each round. The price of NMS Credits increased from £1,850 in Round 1 to £2,300 in Round 2, where it has remained for the two subsequent rounds. Round 3 launched on 2

115 Autumn Statement 2023 speech – GOV.UK (www.gov.uk)

October 2023 with Round 4 opening on 19 February 2024. NE has said that future prices may vary by round and catchment area.

NMS Credits Application Process

1. **Calculate** how many credits your project requires and submit calculations to the LPA; they will confirm your calculations.

2. **Apply for credits** from NE. If your application is successful, you will receive an unsigned certificate and an invoice for 10% of the total cost of the credits you requested. Sign the certificate and send it back to NE along with the payment. You will then receive a countersigned certificate, which can be used as part of your planning application.

3. **Apply for planning permission.** You must receive planning permission within 36 weeks of receiving your certificate. You must let NE know within 8 weeks of receiving your planning confirmation. They will invoice you for the remaining 90% of your credits. Once they have received payment, they will then send you your final certificate.

4. **Submit** your final certificate to your LPA. Once the LPA has confirmed that you have met the nutrient mitigation conditions of your planning application, the housing on your development can be occupied.

The Legal Landscape of Nutrient Neutrality Going Forward

Following the Levelling-up and Regeneration Act 2023 (**LURA**) coming into force, new nutrient pollution standards have been put in place in relation to certain sewage disposal works[116] which are to be achieved (by way of upgrades) by 1 April 2030. Part of this process includes enabling

116 i.e. wastewater treatment works serving a population equivalent over 2,000.

the Secretary of State to designate certain habitat site[117] catchments areas as sensitive for nitrogen and/or phosphorus under the Water Industry Act 1991.[118]

On 25 January 2024, the Secretary of State for the Environment, Food and Rural Affairs duly designated 16 catchments (**Sensitive Catchment Areas**) in which water companies are required to upgrade wastewater treatment works before 1 April 2030.[119]

Upgrading of treatment works

The upgrading of wastewater treatment works within the Sensitive Catchment Areas, which discharge into the protected watercourses, is to ensure that effluent is within acceptable limits (being not more than 10mg/l for nitrogen and 0.25mg/l for phosphorus). The deadline for upgrading is 1 April 2030.

As explained previously, these upgrading works will be factored into any HRA, thereby reducing or eliminating, in time, the need for additional mitigation through the purchase of nutrient credits or other measures.

These measures were the Government's response to calls from developers to reduce the nutrient neutrality burden, which has been hampering development in some areas of the country. Nutrient neutrality has been in the political crosshairs since its inception and developers see it as a time consuming barrier to new houses which don't contribute as much nutrient pollution as other sectors.

---

117 i.e. those in unfavourable condition by virtue of nutrient pollution.

118 Water Industry Act 1991 (as amended by LURA), Sections 96C(1) and (2). As per s.96C(9), *In this section "catchment area", in relation to a habitats site, means the area where water, if released, would drain into the site.*

119 https://www.local.gov.uk/pas/topics/environment/nutrient-neutrality-and-planning-system

Environmentalists regard it as a useful tool which ensures that new development does not contribute to an already significant pollution problem. Offering a solution are those involved in the private market for nutrient credits generated by taking land out of agricultural production or utilising other mitigation strategies.

Developers have asserted that 100,000 new homes are currently being held up by the requirement for nutrient neutrality whilst others have argued that this statistic does not take account of the maturity of the private nutrient credit market which was becoming established.

The Government tabled amendments to (what was then) the Levelling Up and Regeneration Bill ("**LURB**") on 29 August which would change the Habitats Regulations so that nutrient pollution from housing developments would no longer be part of the planning process.

These changes would have been made possible by a new clause in the LURB at 159A which would have given the Secretary of State wide powers to publish regulations which "may make any provision the Secretary of State considers appropriate" about the operation of any "relevant enactment." That definition includes any domestic legislation or retained direct EU legislation relating to the environment so the winds of change may strengthen.

As a result, an appropriate assessment under the Council Directive 92/43/EEC on the Conservation of Natural Habitats and Wild Flora and Fauna ("**EU Habitats Directive**") would no longer have been required.

The amendments would have to have reversed the current position, established in *C G Fry v Secretary of State*[120], where the High Court determined that the relevant provisions of the Habitats Directive remain part of UK law due to the European Union (Withdrawal) Act 2018 ("**Withdrawal Act 2018**").

---

120 [2023] EWHC 1622 (Admin)

As nutrient neutrality is a creation of European law, the UK's withdrawal from the European Union allows the UK Habitats Regulations to transpose the requirements of the EU Habitats Directive. Since Brexit, domestic legislation such as the Habitats Regulations which is derived from EU law continues to have effect pursuant to section 2(1) of the Withdrawal Act 2018. Similarly, the pre-Brexit case law of the CJEU lives on in relation to the interpretation of EU law.

The LURB amendments would have amended the Habitats Regulations if they had not been rejected by the House of Lords. If the Bill had got through both Houses of Parliament then the Government would only be susceptible to Judicial Review if they made decisions in respect of that new legislation which were wrong or unreasonable.

Legal Challenges

It has already become clear that nutrient neutrality (and biodiversity net gain) is seen by opponents of development as a potential Achilles heel providing an opportunity to derail a planning application.

This was certainly the case when Mr. Wyatt challenged the validity of the NE guidance applicable to the Solent, in the case of *R(Wyatt) v Fareham Borough Council.*[121] The High Court decision in that case, to dismiss an application for Judicial Review of the decision to grant planning permission, was then appealed[122] with the Court of Appeal confirming the legality of the 2022 Guidance.

Mr Wyatt is the Chairperson of the Brook Avenue Residents Against Development group which was, as the name implies, not in favour of the proposed development and he judicially reviewed Fareham Borough Council's ("**Council**") decision to grant planning permission. That

[121] *R (Save Warsash and the Western Wards) v Fareham Borough Council* [2021] EWHC 1434 (Admin)

[122] R (Wyatt) v Fareham Borough Council & Natural England [2022] EWCA Civ 983

application for judicial review failed on all fronts but Mr Wyatt obtained permission to appeal that decision and it was this appeal which was considered by the Court of Appeal.

Given their vested interest, NE joined the party and made submissions, as did the landowners of the proposed development site.

The case concerns a planning application for an eight unit development in the catchment area of the Solent and Southampton Water Special Protection Area ("**SPA**").

The Council, as part of the planning process, was required by regulation 63 of the Habitats Regulations to undertake an "appropriate assessment" to ensure that the development would not adversely affect the integrity of the SPA.

Regard was made to the Guidance and a nutrient neutrality budget calculation was carried out.

The case law considered by the Court of Appeal makes it clear that the role of the court is to satisfy itself that the assessment carried out by the Council was lawful and not to undertake an assessment of its own. It is also appropriate for the Council to give significant weight to the advice of an "expert national agency" such as NE.

The Habitats Regulations embody the precautionary principle which requires a high standard of investigation but that does not need to establish an absolute certainty of no adverse effects on the SPA. The test is that the Council must be satisfied that there is no reasonable doubt as to the absence of adverse effects on the integrity of the site concerned. The assessment, using the best scientific knowledge in the field is subjective in nature and the issue ultimately rests on the judgment of the Council.

Natural England Guidance

The 2022 Guidance advocates a nutrient budget which calculates the levels of nutrients produced by a development and compares those to the levels generated by the existing lawful use of the site.

The nutrient loss from the existing use is modelled using standard figures (Farmscoper model) for different types of land use such as agricultural, woodland and green space considering the history of the site over the last 10 years.

If this calculation results in a positive figure, then some form of mitigation is required to avoid increased levels of nutrients in the SPA and the associated problems of algal blooms etc.

In calculating the nutrient output of a development an average national occupancy rate of dwellings of 2.4 persons was used along with maximum daily water usage of 110 litres per person. A 20% precautionary buffer is then applied.

Since the High Court decision referred to above, NE have revised the 2022 Guidance but those changes do not impact on the issues before the Court of Appeal.

Mr Wyatt objected to the use of the average national occupancy rate on the basis that the proposed development was of large detached houses with four or five bedrooms. He also argued that the 20% buffer was an arbitrary figure with no evidential basis.

High Court

The judge was critical of the use of the 2.4 person occupancy rate but did not think it sufficiently unreasonable and that it was in line with the precautionary principle. The reasoning was that there is not a directly proportional link between occupancy and water consumption. Also, the algorithm assumes that the occupants are all inwards migrants to the area and not moving within the locality. The use of the 20% precautionary buffer did not justify judicial intervention as there was room for debate between reasonable scientists.

Court of Appeal

In the leading judgment given by Sir Keith Lindblom, the Senior President of Tribunals, the Court had to determine two questions as to whether the Council had:

- Failed to comply with the Habitats Regulations; and
- Complied with its duty under section 38 (6) of the Planning and Compulsory Purchase Act 2004.

Habitats Regulations

Mr Wyatt criticised the judge for accepting the expert evidence from NE and argued that the failing status of the SPA meant that a greater degree of certainty was required. The uncertain data meant that the approach should have been that of the "reasonable worst-case scenario" which is the approach taken in environmental impact assessments.

The standard occupancy rate was attacked once again and it was argued that the Council should have adopted a bespoke calculation so as to be in accordance with the precautionary principle and based on the best available evidence.

It was also argued that the average figures for agricultural and other land uses were inappropriate as they relied on speculation about future land use and so did not provide the certainty required under regulation 63.

The claimant then attacked the arbitrary nature of the 20% precautionary buffer, with their main points being that it lacked any evidential basis and could only be sensibly quantified once the inherent uncertainty of the scheme had been calculated.

The court rejected these arguments, ruling that the Council had reached an evaluative judgement and the judge had assessed the expert evidence with care. The unfavourable status of the SPA was already acknowledged by the Guidance which the Council relied upon. The judge did not fail to apply the precautionary principle and did not have to assess the "reasonable worst-case scenario." Further, it was open to the Council to rely on the precautionary effect of several factors in the nutrient budget which combined to make the occupancy rate selection acceptable. The High Court's reasoning that there is no directly proportional link between occupancy and water consumption and the algorithm assuming that the occupants are all inwards migrants to the area being cases in point.

The Court said that there is no objection in principle to using standard land use figures and the appropriateness of doing so was a matter of judgement for the Council.

On dealing with the buffer figure of 20% the decision was that it does not lack the necessary certainty merely because it is the product of an exercise of judgment as opposed to an arithmetical calculation.

Planning and Compulsory Purchase Act 2004

Section 38 (6) of the 2004 Act requires a planning application to be determined in accordance with the development plan unless material considerations indicate otherwise. The second question to be determined by the court was whether the Council had complied with this requirement.

Broadly, the Council had acknowledged that it did not meet the five-year housing supply test. As such, development outside defined settlements would be acceptable. The Court accepted that the Council was entitled to conclude that the proposed development was in accordance with the development plan as a whole. That was a matter of judgment when considering two planning policies which pulled in different directions.

Lord Justice Males dissented from the leading judgment on the single issue of the occupancy rate. His view was that the Council's assessment was not in accordance with the Guidance, but the process was lawful because there was a good reason not to follow that procedure.

The reasoning was that the average occupancy rate of 2.4 represents a starting point only and not a mandatory recommendation. Also, for the development in question it was easy to obtain an average occupancy rate for four bedroomed houses (3.14 persons per dwelling) from the same 2011 Census.

Males LJ also argued that the Council erred in assuming that the use of the 2.4 average figure was already sufficiently precautionary, because it assumes that every occupant of every new dwelling is a new resident of the area. That, the judge determined, is not what the Guidance says.

The Council then mistakenly took the view that the application of the 20% precautionary buffer helps ameliorate the effect of underestimating the total population of the development. Again, Males LJ argued that this is not a correct application of the methodology. The precautionary buffer is not a substitute for using the best available evidence-based occupancy rate. It is an additional protection to be applied after the evidence has been gathered for the nutrient budget and that process has been completed.

However, the question for the Council was not whether it had followed the Guidance methodology but whether it had carried out a sufficient "appropriate assessment" for the purposes of the Habitats Regulations. The Guidance is not mandatory and NE said they had no concerns which was a view the Council was entitled to have regard. That was a good reason for departing from the Guidance methodology and so the assessment was lawful.

As a postscript, Males LJ pointed out that the 2022 updated guidance from Natural England recognises that the average occupancy rate of 2.4 may not be appropriate for certain types of development.

C G Fry

The recent case of C G Fry v Secretary of State[123] considered whether the 2022 Guidance applies to developments which already have outline planning consent.

In this case Somerset Council (**Somerset LPA**) had granted outline planning permission for 650 houses, community and commercial use, a primary school and associated infrastructure. As usual, the outline consent was subject to various conditions or reserved matters.

The planning permission was due to be implemented in eight phases with the first two being commenced under separate reserved matters approvals.

In June 2020 the developer, C G Fry (**Claimant**) obtained reserved matters approval for the third phase of 190 dwellings (**Development**). The approval was subject to a number of conditions but none of them related to nutrient neutrality.

In August 2020, the initial NE guidance was published which dropped the nutrient neutrality bombshell onto the desk of all the affected local authorities, including the Somerset LPA. The Development had the potential, adversely, to affect the Somerset Levels and Moors Ramsar Site, so an AA was required. Whilst the Habitats Regulations do not designate Ramsar Sites as protected areas, the National Planning Policy Framework (**NPPF**) grants them the same level of protection.

In June 2021 the Claimant sought discharge of a number of the conditions, none of which went to the principle of the Development, which had been established under the outline planning consent. The Somerset LPA withheld approval on the basis that an AA was needed.

123 C G Fry & Son Limited v Secretary of State for Levelling Up Housing and Communities & Somerset Council [2023] EWHC 1622 Admin

Appeal

In April 2022, the Claimant appealed arguing that an AA was not needed at the discharge of conditions stage or, if it was, it should be confined in scope to matters being considered for the conditions in question.

The Somerset LPA maintained that an AA was needed and their own shadow calculations showed that the Development would have an adverse impact on the Ramsar Site.

The Inspector dismissed the Claimant's appeal finding that the NPPF overarching protection was legitimate as discharge of conditions was part of a wider consent process, which would permit the Development to have an adverse effect on the Ramsar Site. An AA was required at the discharge of conditions stage. The unfulfilled requirement for an AA was an issue of material significance, which outweighed the delay in housing delivery.

Written Ministerial Statement

In July 2022 the Secretary of State for Environment Food and Rural Affairs issued a Written Ministerial Statement which confirmed that "the Habitats Regulations Assessment provisions apply to any consent, permission or other authorisation, this may include post-permission approvals, reserved matters or discharges of conditions."

The Claimant therefore launched this claim for statutory review under section 288 of the Town and Country Planning Act 1990 ("1990 Act.")

Legal Framework

Nutrient neutrality is a creation of European law with the Habitats Regulations transposing the requirements of Council Directive 92/43/EEC on the Conservation of Natural Habitats and Wild Flora and Fauna ("Habitats Directive.")

Prior to Brexit the provisions of the Habitats Directive could be relied upon directly in the English courts to trump domestic law, including the

1990 Act. That reliance is also possible in circumstances in which the wording of the Habitats Regulations fell short of achieving the level of protection required.

The Court of Justice of the European Union ("CJEU") adopts a strict precautionary approach to the assessment provisions of the Habitats Directive, so authorities have to make certain that development will not adversely affect protected sites.

Further, the CJEU held in the Dutch Nitrogen Case (which prompted the Natural England advice note referred to above) that the AA must be capable of removing all reasonable scientific doubt as to the effects of development on a protected site.

Since Brexit, domestic legislation derived from EU law, such as the Habitats Regulations, continues to have effect pursuant to section 2(1) of the European Union (Withdrawal) Act 2018 ("EU Withdrawal Act"). Similarly, the pre-Brexit case law of the CJEU lives on in relation to the interpretation of EU law.

Case law (drawing on examples relating to environmental impact assessments) has established that an AA can be carried out at the reserved matters stage.

Grounds of Challenge

The Claimant's case was that the additional phosphate loading, caused by the Development, was irrelevant, as it fell outside the matters left to be determined in a planning context after the grant of the outline permission. In addition, none of the conditions associated with the reserved matters application related to the phosphate issue.

The first line of attack from the Claimant was that the Habitats Regulations only apply to the formal grant of planning permission and not the approval of reserved matters or discharge of conditions. The Judge agreed with this strict interpretation but found that the AA requirements applied due to Article 6 (3) of the Habitats Directive, a purposive interpretation of their provisions and case law binding him.

Habitats Directive – Article 6 (3)

The Claimant argued that the Habitats Directive had no status in the UK legal system as there was no EU or UK case law dating from before Brexit. The Judge disagreed with that view confirming that Article 6 (3) remains part of UK law. This is due to it having been accepted as binding by the CJEU in a previous case, as it was closely related to another provision of the Habitats Directive, which was the key clause in that case. This is because the EU Withdrawal Act states that previous case law will be recognised "whether or not as an essential part of the decision in the case."

Article 6 (3) requires that an AA must be carried out before a planning project is approved. A planning consent is part of agreeing a project when it consists of implementing development. In turn, the discharge of pre-commencement conditions is a necessary step in the implementation of development. In the Fry case the conditions could not be discharged without an AA being undertaken.

Purposive Interpretation

The Habitats Regulations demand a purposive interpretation so that they apply to subsequent consent stages such as reserved matters applications and discharge of conditions. This approach stems from the strict precautionary approach which the CJEU has adopted to the assessment provisions of the Habitats Directive.

The Claimant's case was that the precautionary approach is already observed as the 2017 Regulations require an assessment at the outline stage "whether before or after obtaining approval of any reserved matters." Leaving aside the obvious timing issue in this case (that the NE advice note was issued after the grant of outline permission) the Judge identified the potential for negative environmental issues only surfacing after the initial stages of a multi-stage planning process. It must be remembered that in such a multi-stage process there is no implementing decision until the reserved matters are approved and conditions discharged. This is because any development in breach of such requirements is unlawful.

Caselaw

The Judge's view was that existing caselaw provided authority for the proposition that an AA can apply at the reserved matters or discharge of conditions stage, even if there has been a grant of outline planning permission under which the subsequent approval is the implementing decision. All the cases concerned the interpretation of the Habitats Directive and the Habitats Regulations and the point that the facts were different was no basis for undermining the principles they established.

Any arguments that the Habitats Regulations must be subservient to the 1990 Act is met by the long-established principle of the superiority of EU law over domestic UK legislation, which is preserved by the EU Withdrawal Act.

Conclusion & leapfrog appeal

The conclusion is that the Habitats Directive and the Habitats Regulations mandate that an AA must be undertaken before a project is consented, regardless of the stage it has reached.

An interesting postscript to this case is that permission was given for a leapfrog appeal straight from the High Court, bypassing the Court of Appeal, to the Supreme Court. This is a rare event and reserved for the cases of the highest public interest. By way of illustration, the last example was the Brexit challenge brought by Gina Miller.

On 24 August 2023, the Supreme Court refused permission to appeal on the ground that the case is not suitable for a leapfrog appeal. An expedited appeal to the Court of Appeal is the consolation prize and the hearing took place on 19 and 20 March 2024. The decision is due after the publication of this book and will be eagerly awaited by all involved in nutrient neutrality schemes.

CHAPTER FIVE

THE CORPORATE MARKET

Shareholders and Stakeholders

Are corporations primarily beholden to their shareholders or to society at large? For-profit corporations certainly have an obligation to generate value for its shareholders. How it does so is decided by its directors, who in the UK hold a fiduciary duty to exercise reasonable care, skill and diligence when carrying out their responsibilities.[124] However, a corporation's activities impact many more people than its shareholders, such as its suppliers, customers, employees and possibly entire communities; this wider group is known collectively as "stakeholders." What obligations does a corporation have when managing the interests of shareholders and stakeholders should they come into conflict?

For many years, legal scholars suggested that shareholder primacy was not only the norm, but "the most fundamental concept in corporate law and corporate governance."[125] However, this theory has come under criticism for failing to take externalities—costs created by a producer but not borne by that producer—into consideration. Consider a manufacturing firm that dumps toxic byproducts into a local river; its shareholders will benefit from saving the costs of proper waste disposal while avoiding the

124 Section 174 Companies Act 2006

125 Rhee, Robert J., A Legal Theory of Shareholder Primacy (March 21, 2017). 102 Minnesota Law Review, 2017 (Forthcoming), University of Florida Levin College of Law Research Paper No. 17-20, Available at SSRN: https://ssrn.com/abstract=2938806

direct consequences of this decision unless they live downriver from the factory.

In response, governments and legal scholars have developed more holistic approaches to corporate governance. After much debate, in 2008 the UK adopted what it called the Enlightened Shareholder Value (ESV) principle which it deployed primarily through section 172 of the Companies Act 2006. The ESV principle seeks to strike a compromise between shareholder primacy and stakeholder theory by positing it is in the long-term interest of shareholders for directors to ensure the firm is operating in a sustainable and well-reputed manner. As such, s172 requires directors to have regard to the interests of certain stakeholders when making decisions. Large companies must publish an annual statement describing how the firm's directors are complying with this requirement.[126] The s172 duty is subjective, meaning a director need only honestly believe they are complying with the duty for it to be discharged.[127] In all, the manner in which the government applied the ESV principle received a decidedly mixed reception amongst legal academics and did not quell calls for greater scrutiny of corporate obligations to society.[128]

Why corporates are under pressure to change

Corporate Social Responsibility

Corporate social responsibility (CSR) is a form of business self-regulation in which firms voluntarily dedicate resources to improve the social spheres in which they operate. CSR is a broad concept which can range

---

[126] Section 414CZA Companies Act 2006

[127] *Re Smith and Fawcett Ltd.* [1942] Ch 304

[128] Attenborough, D. (2013). [Review of The Enlightened Shareholder Value Principle and Corporate Governance, by A. Keay]. The Modern Law Review, 76(5), 940–943. http://www.jstor.org/stable/24029746

from charitable contributions and pro-bono work to repositioning a firm's entire business model to ensure more sustainable practices.

Proponents argue that a robust CSR strategy can benefit a firm in many different ways. Externally, a successful CSR campaign can enhance a firm's reputation, which can in turn increase consumer confidence and enhance brand premiums. Internally, employees may be more motivated to work harder knowing that the firm they are operating for aligns with and supports their personal values. Increasingly, it is also helping firms differentiate themselves in extremely competitive recruitment markets. An industry of third-party auditors and certifiers have sprung up to verify a business' CSR credentials.

Examples

- **B Corp.** B Corp is a social impact certificate offered by B Lab, a nonprofit organization, to for-profit corporations. To qualify, a corporation must pass a 200-question assessment on the corporation's business model, operations and impact on stakeholders. B-Corps must also modify their company's constitution to include a commitment to consider stakeholder interests when making business decisions. Following certification, B Corps must publish an annual impact report and recertify every three years.[129]

- **Planet Mark.** PlanetMark is a Welsh for-profit corporation[130] that offers sustainability certifications to other businesses. To be certified, a business must provide evidence of quantifiable sustainability performance, publicly commit to reducing emissions and engage with relevant stakeholders on

---

129 B Labs, "The B Corp Certification Process," https://pardot.bcorporation.net/l/39792/2023-02-07/9rblgc/39792/1675785775pOkvYjFy/Guide_to_the_B_Corp_Certification_Process.pdf

130 Companies House, "Planet First Limited" https://find-and-update.company-information.service.gov.uk/company/08472139

sustainability, and achieve a minimum level of improvement every year.[131]

Environmental, Social and Corporate Governance Investment

Firms with a solid and credible CSR strategy may also be attractive to a particular type of investor. In 2002, the then-United Nations Secretary General Kofi Annan invited eighteen financial institutions from 9 countries to "develop guidelines and recommendations on how to better integrate environmental, social and corporate governance issues in asset management, securities brokerage services and associated research institutions."[132] The resulting report formed the foundations of Environmental, Social and Corporate Governance (ESG) investment, an investment philosophy in which investors broaden their considerations beyond return on investment to include a wider spectrum of criteria such as a firm's environmental impact. ESG funding may only be available to firms that meet environmental, social or corporate governance thresholds set out in the fund mandate.

Examples

- **ESG Funds.** Asset managers have launched hundreds of ESG funds to capture investor appetite for sustainable investment; total ESG fund assets under management reached US$37.8 trillion as of 2021; Bloomberg estimates that ESG assets may grow to be a third of total global assets under management by

131 PlanetMark, "Business Certification Scheme: Rules, Procedures and management." https://www.planetmark.com/wp-content/uploads/2021/12/PMBusinessCertificationSchemeRulesProceduresandManagement.pdf

132 "Who cares wins: connecting financial markets to a changing world (English)." Washington, D.C.: World Bank Group. http://documents.worldbank.org/curated/en/280911488968799581/Who-cares-wins-connecting-financial-markets-to-a-changing-world

2025.[133] ESG funds each have a different specialty—some are region- or industry-specific, while others invest in large-cap multinationals. Many private and government-backed venture capital funds exclusively invest in start-ups with ESG business models. As there is no central regulatory definition for what ESG investment consists of, each fund will often have their own parameters for what ESG targets need to be met for the company to fall within the scope of the fund. In March 2023, the Government published a consultation paper seeking input on establishing a regulatory regime for ESG ratings, but as of writing no further progress has been made.[134]

- **Government funding.** World governments have also opened multiple funds to subsidize ESG investment. Many funds and incentives are covered elsewhere in this book, such as nutrient neutrality and biodiversity net gain schemes. In 2021, the UK Department for Business, Energy & Industrial Strategy launched the "Net Zero Innovation Portfolio," a £1 billion fund set up in order to "decrease the costs of decarbonisation and set the UK on the path to a low carbon future."[135] This includes contribution to the Clean Growth Fund, a venture capital fund co-funded by the UK government and its private sector.[136]

---

133 Bloomberg, ESG assets may hit $53 trillion by 2025, a third of global AUM

134 Gov.uk, "Future regulatory regime for ESG ratings providers," https://www.gov.uk/government/consultations/future-regulatory-regime-for-environmental-social-and-governance-esg-ratings-providers

135 Gov.uk, "Net Zero Innovation Portfolio," https://www.gov.uk/government/collections/net-zero-innovation-portfolio

136 Gov.uk, "Clean Growth Fund," https://www.gov.uk/government/publications/clean-growth-equity-fund

Legislative and regulatory compliance

Along with carrots to incentivize sustainable business practices, the UK government has also been rolling out additional reporting and compliance legislation to disincentivize unsustainable practices.

In 2013, the Secretary of State issued a statutory instrument[137] requiring firms to report information on greenhouse gas (GHG) emissions in their Directors' Reports. GHG emissions are calculated using standards established by the Greenhouse Gas Protocol,[138] a globally-recognized accounting standard. The Protocol divides emissions into three groups, which it calls "scopes":

- **Scope 1:** Emissions originating directly from an organization, e.g. the fuel used by a company vehicle.
- **Scope 2:** Emissions for which the organization causes indirectly, e.g. the CO2 cost of the electricity consumed by the organization.
- **Scope 3:** All other emissions for which the organization is indirectly responsible across its value chain, e.g. emissions made by the products it manufactures.

In 2022, the Secretary of State issued two statutory instruments mandating that certain firms[139] and limited liability partnerships[140] must issue annual sustainability information statements; these statements must

137 The Companies Act 2006 (Strategic Report and Directors' Report) Regulations 2013, https://www.legislation.gov.uk/uksi/2013/1970/contents/made

138 Greenhouse Gas Protocol, https://ghgprotocol.org/about-us

139 The Companies (Strategic Report) (Climate-related Financial Disclosure) Regulations 2022, https://www.legislation.gov.uk/uksi/2022/31/made

140 The Limited Liability Partnerships (Strategic Report) (Climate-related Financial Disclosure) Regulations 2022, https://www.legislation.gov.uk/uksi/2022/46/introduction/made

identify environmental risks affecting the company's operations and how the firm is managing said risks.

Understanding the corporate market

Between stakeholder pressure, financing pressure and legislative pressure it should come as no surprise that a wide range of services have sprung up to ensure corporates maximize their sustainable practices and minimize their environmental footprint. It would be impossible to delve into the myriad of CSR services available to corporates in detail; instead, this section will focus on three markets that tend to be the largest factors in a UK firm's CSR strategy: waterway infrastructure, supply chains and the direct ESG market.

The Waterway Infrastructure Market

Effective and hygienic waterway management has moved up as a Government priority in recent years. In April 2023, DEFRA published a policy paper entitled "Plan for Water: our integrated plan for delivering clean and plentiful water."[141] The paper is meant to provide a pathway for achieving the Government's goal of improving access to clean and plentiful water as part of its Environmental Improvement Plan 2023.[142] The Water Plan seeks to reform management of the UK's entire water system to deploy a "systemic, local, catchment-based approach" [143] to tackling water pollution which "considers all pressures in the round, rather than in isolation."[144]

---

[141] https://www.gov.uk/government/publications/plan-for-water-our-integrated-plan-for-delivering-clean-and-plentiful-water/plan-for-water-our-integrated-plan-for-delivering-clean-and-plentiful-water

[142] https://www.gov.uk/government/publications/environmental-improvement-plan/environmental-improvement-plan-2023-executive-summary

[143] Plan for Water, "Ministerial Forward."

[144] Ibid, "Integrated approach across catchments."

The UK water management industry is organized via catchments—river basins over which water utility firms have responsibility following the privatization of the industry in 1989.[145] The goal of the Government's catchment-based approach is to tackle pollution issues at their source, rather than in the last steps of the water distribution supply chain: it is cheaper to pay a farmer to move their livestock elsewhere than to pay for a filter system to clean up the water pollution caused by said livestock. This holistic approach includes both catchment action plans and catchment-scale partnerships to "coordinate action and investment where rivers need it most."[146]

Examples

- **Bristol Avon Catchment Partnership** is co-hosted by Wessex Water and the West of England Rural Network. The Bristol Avon waterway has been degraded by agricultural and urban run-off along with hundreds of weirs, walls and culverts. The goal of the partnership is to provide a platform to explore holistic solutions to the issue and funding to put those solutions into practice. As of April 2023, the Partnership has funded 44 projects with £230,000 in direct funding and £326,000 in secured match funding by other organisations. According to DEFRA, the success of these projects has led to "further investment in excess of £7 million."[147]

Supply Chain Market

As highlighted previously in this chapter, environmental sustainability reporting often extends beyond a firm's activities to include all steps within a product's supply chain. This puts pressure on firms not just to

[145] Thames Water, "Our catchment management initiatives." https://www.thameswater.co.uk/about-us/responsibility/smarter-water-catchments

[146] Plan for Water, "Transform management of the whole water system."

[147] Plan for Water, "Case study: Bristol Avon Catchment Partnership"

ensure sustainable practices within their operations but also to work with suppliers and clients that are equally committed to sustainable initiatives. Cutting supply chain emissions can go a long way to reducing a firm's carbon footprint: a 2016 McKinsey report found that 90% of consumer goods companies' environmental impact comes from their supply chains[148], while a 2019 report from the environmental charity CDP concludes that "supply chain emissions are on average 5.5 times as high as a corporation's direct emissions."[149] It is therefore understandable that, of the 239 companies that signed up to the Science Based Targets Initiative in 2020 (an initiative launched to develop emissions reduction targets for companies in line with climate science), 94% made commitments to reduce emissions from both suppliers and customers.[150]

Of course, reducing supply chain emissions is easier said than done as firms do not have direct control over their suppliers. As with any commercial negotiation, leverage is a key component: the bigger a firm's presence in a supply chain, the more suppliers and clients will have to acquiesce to the firm's demands. An example from the agricultural sector is the significant influence that supermarkets have over their farmer suppliers. This has led to sustainability targets and price linkages being included in purchase contracts. Incentives can take the form of carrots (public recognition and increased business with suppliers that follow sustainable guidelines) or sticks (refusal to do business with suppliers that do not meet certain standards). In 2017, Nestlé launched an initiative with its UK dairy suppliers in which the global food behemoth would

148 Anne-Titia Bové and Steven Swartz, "Starting at the source: Sustainability in supply chains," *McKinsey* 11 Nov 2016 https://www.mckinsey.com/capabilities/sustainability/our-insights/starting-at-the-source-sustainability-in-supply-chains

149 "Supply chains hold the key to one gigaton of emissions savings, finds new report," 09 Dec 2019 https://www.cdp.net/en/articles/media/supply-chains-hold-the-key-to-one-gigaton-of-emissions-savings-finds-new-report

150 Peter Spiller, "Making supply-chain decarbonization happen," *McKinsey* 14 June 2021 https://www.mckinsey.com/capabilities/operations/our-insights/making-supply-chain-decarbonization-happen

pay a per-litre premium to milk farmers that took measures to improve biodiversity and watercourse protection on their farms.[151]

A report from the Economist Intelligence Institute[152] divides the techniques firms can use to hold suppliers accountable into seven categories:

- **Scoring.** Firms with a choice of suppliers may issue supplier scorecards and offer business to those with a better score. The report notes that "scoring systems are most effective when the future of the relationship with the supplier is at stake."

- **Public targets.** Some firms mandate that their suppliers set and work towards emissions-related targets, such as waste reduction or the use of more energy-efficient technologies. Others set general emissions-reduction targets and leave it to the firms to develop a strategy to achieve the set target.

- **Industry collaboration.** Depending on the industry, collaboration between buyers can force suppliers to meet certain standards. Collaborations such as the Sustainable Natural Rubber Initiative[153] produce industry standards such as a standardized verification system for suppliers to demonstrate best practices.

- **Technology.** Deploying even small technological improvements across a supply chain—e.g. tracking goods to develop a more

---

151 Natural Capital Impact Group, "Modelling better business: Nestlé trials natural capital premium with UK dairy farmers." https://www.cisl.cam.ac.uk/system/files/documents/modelling-better-business-case-study-feb-2018.pdf

152 *Economist Intelligence Unit*, "Sustainability: The Missing Link" https://impact.econ-asia.com/perspectives/sustainability/sustainability-missing-link

153 https://www.rubberstudy.org/snr-i

fuel-efficient method of distribution—can lead to significant downstream gains given the scale of modern logistics networks.

- **Awards.** Certain firms have used awards to incentivize supplier behavior. These awards can build a supplier's prestige, encouraging suppliers to compete in developing innovative methods to improve sustainability.

- **Advising suppliers.** Firms can also advise their suppliers on how to improve sustainability. A collaborative approach—such as hosting workshops or sending experts out to review and suggest improvements to a supplier's operations—can help suppliers meet the higher demands made by their clients.

- **Reverse logistics** is the practice of moving goods upstream through a supply chain. A common example is sending packaging back to the supplier for reuse. This is a growing trend in manufacturing: the Economist report notes that 36% of surveyed respondents incorporate some form of reverse logistics within their supply chains.

Direct Investment

Many firms are improving their sustainability credentials by investing directly into CSR projects. Direct investments are typically made via assisting non-profits that advance a firm's CSR objectives. This can be via funding or providing equipment and expertise. Some firms might set up their own projects—in 2020, the multinational beer and real estate firm BrewDog purchased a 9,300-acre plot of land in the Scottish Highlands for reforestation with the goal of creating "the single largest native woodland establishment and peatland restoration project ever in the UK, capable of pulling one million tonnes of carbon dioxide out of the atmosphere."[154] In 2023, insurance giant Aviva announced a £38m commitment to restore the UK's rapidly-dwindling temperate rainforests.[155]

Other firms devote their expertise assisting existing nonprofit organisations. Professional services firms such as accountancies, law firms and consultancies often have pro-bono programs in which their staff volunteer their working hours to nonprofits. Examples include:

- **Partnership for Forests**, a UK nonprofit that supports public-private reforestation partnerships and promote sustainable forestry in deforestation hotspots around the globe.[156] This support ranges from securing the partnership and permitting necessary to get a project off the ground to ensuring sustainable harvesting practices. The nonprofit is funded by the UK Foreign Commonwealth and Development Office with technical assistance from systems designer SYSTEMIQ and The Palladium Group, a global consulting firm.

- **UNESCO Man and Biosphere Programme** is a biodiversity conservation initiative that focuses on innovation and testing new conservation strategies via their Biosphere Reserves Network of 748 biosphere reserves across 134 countries.[157] Biosphere reserves are sites in which ecological sustainability theories are tested to determine real-world practicality and scalability. In 2022,

---

[154] James Watt Brewdog, "BrewDog's Lost Forest Project: Understanding the Vision and Impact." https://jameswattbrewdog.com/brewdogs-lost-forest-project-understanding-the-vision-and-impact/

[155] Aviva, "Aviva helps restore rare native British rainforests." https://www.aviva.com/newsroom/news-releases/2023/02/aviva-helps-restore-rare-native-british-rainforests/

[156] Partnership for Forests, "What We Do," https://partnershipsforforests.com/what-we-do/

[157] UNESCO, "World Network of Biosphere Reserves," https://en.unesco.org/biosphere/wnbr

German appliance conglomerate Siemens partnered with the North Devon UNESCO Biosphere Reserve in South West England to improve the biosphere's digital infrastructure by developing a natural capital marketplace and enhance the biosphere's environmental monitoring technology.[158]

[158] Siemens, "Biosphere Foundation partners with Siemens to accelerate digital transformation of natural capital sector", https://news.siemens.co.uk/news/biosphere-foundation-partners-with-siemens-to-accelerate-digital-transformation-of-natural-capital-sector

CHAPTER SIX

AGRICULTURAL MARKET & ELMS

Introduction

European Union members adhere to a Common Agricultural Policy (CAP) set by the European Commission. The EU CAP is broadly divided into two pillars: the "agricultural guarantee" pillar which comprises agricultural subsidies and ensures a common organization of member-state agricultural markets, and the "agricultural structural policy" pillar which focuses on rural development.[159]

Following the UK's exit from the EU, the government was tasked with providing a comprehensive domestic system to replace CAP. DEFRA has effected this transition through Environmental Land Management (ELM) schemes, a web of financial incentives meant to support agricultural production, improve rural infrastructure and encourage environmentally-friendly agricultural practices.[160]

There are three broad ELM schemes: Sustainable Farming Incentive (SFI), Countryside Stewardship (CS) and Landscape Recovery (LR). SFI and CS amount to a list of actions that can be undertaken by a landowner that will be rewarded by payments from DEFRA. LR schemes are

---

159 European Commission, "Common Agricultural Policy funds," https://agriculture.ec.europa.eu/common-agricultural-policy/financing-cap/cap-funds_en

160 DEFRA ELMS policy paper, https://www.gov.uk/government/publications/environmental-land-management-update-how-government-will-pay-for-land-based-environment-and-climate-goods-and-services/environmental-land-management-elm-update-how-government-will-pay-for-land-based-environment-and-climate-goods-and-services

bespoke agreements struck between a landowner (or group of landowners) and DEFRA.

- **Sustainable Farming Incentive.** SFI financially incentivizes farmers who agree to undertake sustainable agricultural practices on their farm, such as producing a soil management plan and placing grass buffer strips on arable land.[161]

- **Countryside Stewardship.** CS schemes finance and incentivize more substantial environmental commitments that may require initial capital investments.[162] CS provides grants for projects such as tree planting and flood mitigation on permanent grassland.

    - **CS Plus** is a subsection of the CS strategy aimed at collaborative projects that will "reward farmers for taking coordinating action"[163] with regard to environmental protection; details of the scheme have not yet been released at time of writing.

---

161 NFU, "SFI – scheme guidance and information," 10 Jan 2024 https://www.nfuonline.com/updates-and-information/sfi-scheme-guidance-and-information/

162 Government guidance. "Countryside Stewardship: get funding to protect and improve the land you manage." https://www.gov.uk/guidance/countryside-stewardship-get-funding-to-protect-and-improve-the-land-you-manage

163 Government press release. "Thérèse Coffey: Farmers central to food production and environmental action" Jan 26 2023 https://www.gov.uk/government/news/therese-coffey-farmers-central-to-food-production-and-environmental-action

- **Landscape Recovery.** LR schemes are suitable for large-scale, long-term environmental projects such as peatland or habitat restoration.[164]

In January 2024, DEFRA announced several reforms to the ELMS regime:[165]

- Payments for SFI and CS schemes will increase by an average of 10%

- 50 new ELMS action opportunities

- Higher premiums paid towards actions classified as higher priority by the government

- SFI and mid-tier CS application process will be merged and accepted on a rolling basis from the summer of 2024.[166]

<u>Sustainable Farming Incentive</u>

SFI agreements last three years. Payments are made quarterly; the more actions a farmer commits to, the larger the payment. The scope of SFI has grown over the past several years to include eight areas[167]:

---

164 DEFRA policy paper, "Landscape Recovery: Round Two." 18 May 2023 https://www.gov.uk/government/publications/landscape-recovery-more-information-on-how-the-scheme-will-work/landscape-recovery-round-2

165 https://defrafarming.blog.gov.uk/2024/01/04/environmental-land-management-in-2024-details-of-actions-and-payments/

166 NFU, "SFI expansion welcome but deliverability questions remain," 04 Jan 2024 https://www.nfuonline.com/updates-and-information/sfi-2024-expansion-revealed-at-ofc-2024/

167 https://www.gov.uk/government/collections/sustainable-farming-incent ive-guidance

- Soil health
- Moorlands
- Hedgerows
- Integrated pest management
- Nutrient management
- Farmland wildlife
- Buffer strips
- Low input grassland

Actions may range from regular assessment and production of a soil management plan (annual payment of £95 plus £5.80 per hectare)[168] to providing winter bird food on arable and horticultural land (£732 per hectare per year).[169] Landowners should inspect the menu of available actions carefully to decide which might be most suitable for them.

Eligibility[170,171]

Currently, only farmers that are eligible for a Basic Payment Scheme may qualify for SFI as their details are already registered with the RPA. This requirement is likely to eventually be dropped as the scheme continues to expand. The land must be wholly located in England and the applicant

---

168 https://www.gov.uk/guidance/sfi-actions-for-soils

169 https://www.gov.uk/guidance/sfi-actions-for-farmland-wildlife-on-arable-and-horticultural-land

170 https://www.gov.uk/guidance/what-to-do-before-you-apply-for-an-sfi-agreement

171 https://www.gov.uk/guidance/what-land-is-eligible-for-an-sfi-agreement

is expected to have management control over the land for the three-year duration of the SFI agreement. More specific requirements might be necessary depending on the action for which the farmer is applying (e.g. for hedgerows, applicants must have control on both sides of the hedgerow).

Application process

Applications are made via the government's Rural Payments Service online platform.[172] A step-by-step guide is available in the government application guidance.[173]

Countryside Stewardship

CS provides financial incentives for 260 actions; these actions can be found via the UK Government Countryside Stewardship grant finder.[174] Payments are administered through grants administered by the Rural Payments Agency (RPA). Each grant has different eligibility criteria and can fund different actions; applicants may apply for multiple grants simultaneously. Each action will have their own application and monitoring requirements. If an application is successful, the applicant will receive an agreement offer. Once that agreement is accepted, they enter into an agreement with RPA.

Grants

For all grants, owner occupiers, tenants, landlords and certain licensors may apply. Applicant must have management control of the land. Land parcels must be entirely within England.

---

172 https://www.gov.uk/claim-rural-payments

https://assets.publishing.service.gov.uk/media/65365d2c26b9b1000daf1d73/SFI23_how_to_apply_for_an_SFI_agreement_V.2.pdf

174 https://www.gov.uk/countryside-stewardship-grants

The applicable grants are:

- **Mid-Tier:**[175] A mid-tier grant supports a range of activities from annual multi-year management agreements to one-off payments for specific capital works. Mid-tier grants are used to achieve one or more of four specific environmental benefits: air quality; water quality; natural flood management; and boundaries, trees and orchards.
    - **Wildlife Offers** are a subsection of Mid-Tier that focus on providing farm wildlife habitats. The application process is non-competitive and quicker than general Mid-Tier grants.
- **Higher Tier:**[176] Similar to mid-tier, but the projects in question require more complex and longer-term management, such as woodland improvement or habitat restoration.
- **Capital Grants:**[177] Three-year agreements for capital items that achieve the same objectives set out in Mid-Tier. Capital grants may also be used to support other schemes such as SFI.
- **Higher Tier Capital Grants:**[178] Three-year agreements for capital items. HTCG are standalone grants to achieve additional environmental benefits without the need for a Higher Tier agreement.

---

175 https://www.gov.uk/government/publications/mid-tier-grants-and-wildlife-offers-2023-countryside-stewardship/applicants-guide-mid-tier-grants-and-wildlife-offers-2023

176 https://www.gov.uk/government/publications/higher-tier-grants-2023-countryside-stewardship/applicants-guide-higher-tier-grants-2023

177 https://www.gov.uk/government/publications/capital-grants-2024/applicants-guide-capital-grants-2024--2

178 https://www.gov.uk/government/publications/higher-tier-capital-grants-2024/applicants-guide-higher-tier-capital-grants-2024

- **Implementation Plan and Feasibility Study Agreements:**[179] Grants specifically to fund implementation plans and feasibility studies in conjunction with Mid-tier or Higher tier grants. Must have approval from a Natural England advisor before applying.

- **Woodland Management Plan Grants:**[180] A one-off payment to create a 10-year woodland management plan. The plan must be fully compliant with the UK Forestry Standard.[181]

- **Protection and Infrastructure Grants**[182] are standalone capital grants for woodland infrastructure capital items, beaver protection capital items and/or beaver dam management capital items.

- **Woodland Tree Health (WTH) Grants:**[183] These grants are divided into the WTH Restoration grant, which supports restocking woodland after felling due to tree health; and the WTH improvement grant, which supports the removal of infected trees. The grants may be applied for individually or together. WTH grants are not competitive.

---

179 https://www.gov.uk/government/publications/implementation-plan-pa1-and-feasibility-study-pa2-application-form/how-to-apply-for-an-implementation-plan-or-feasibility-study-capital-grant

180 https://www.gov.uk/government/publications/woodland-management-plan-grants-2024/applicants-guide-woodland-management-plan-grant-2024--2

181 https://www.gov.uk/government/publications/the-uk-forestry-standard

182 https://www.gov.uk/government/publications/protection-and-infrastructure-grants-2024/applicants-guide-protection-and-infrastructure-grants-2024

183 https://www.gov.uk/government/publications/woodland-tree-health-grants-2024/applicants-guide-woodland-tree-health-grants-2024--2

- **Facilitation Fund:**[184] This fund supports individuals who coordinate between different groups of farmers, foresters and other land managers to develop environmental improvements. Individuals with suitable environmental land management experience and facilitation skills may apply to become a CS facilitator. This will likely be folded into the CS Plus subsection once details of the scheme are published.

Sample Countryside Stewardship Action

AB11: Cultivated areas for arable plants[185]

- **Pay:** £660 per hectare

- **Grant:** CS Mid Tier and Higher Tier.

- **Objective:** Create uncropped, cultivated areas for a wide range of scarce and declining arable plants, allowing them to increase their populations over time.

- **Prohibitions:** Land manager may not:

    - Disturb cultivated areas

    - Apply any fertilisers or manures

    - Apply any lime

    - Use any pesticides (except for herbicides for the control of injurious weeds)

---

184 https://www.gov.uk/government/publications/facilitation-fund-2024-countryside-stewardship/applicants-guide-facilitation-fund-2024

185 https://www.gov.uk/countryside-stewardship-grants/cultivated-areas-for-arable-plants-ab11

- **Requirements:**
  - Whole or part parcel
  - Rotational
  - Only on arable land
    - Where evidence or records exist for important arable plants, or
    - Where the land is part of the Wild Pollinator and Farm Wildlife Package
- **Records:** Keep records at parcel level of field operations; take photographs.

<u>Landscape Recovery</u>

Landscape Recovery (LR) programs are bespoke, long-term and large-scale projects submitted by land managers and approved by DEFRA. The Government highlighted four distinguishing features[186] of the scheme:

- **Large-scale projects:** LR projects are meant to deliver outcomes that require collaboration across a large area, such as landscape ecological restoration.
- **Long-term public funding**: LR projects will take 20 years or longer to deliver on the project objectives.

---

186 https://www.gov.uk/government/publications/landscape-recovery-more-information-on-how-the-scheme-will-work/landscape-recovery-round-2#overview

- **Bespoke agreements**: The project should be specific to the locality and difficult to replicate through other schemes.

- **Blended funding**: While LR project development may be initially financed through public funding, the plan should be robust enough to secure private funding during its development phase.

The selection process for LR funding is competitive: applications are considered in rounds and scored against standard criteria which differ depending on which environmental objectives DEFRA seeks to focus on for the round in question. The highest scoring projects will receive funding. New guidelines are published for each round. As of writing, two rounds of applications have been completed, and the third round has yet to be announced. [187]

For round two, Landscape Recovery schemes were divided into five phases:

- **Application**, the window in which applications may be submitted

- **Evaluation,** during which applications are considered. Up to 25 of the highest-scoring projects will advance to the next round.

- **Enrolment**, a 10–14 week window wherein further background checks are conducted on the successful applicants culminating in a project development grant offer.

---

[187] Gov.uk Policy Paper, "Landscape Recovery: how the schemes will work," https://www.gov.uk/government/publications/landscape-recovery-more-information-on-how-the-scheme-will-work

- **Project development,**[188] a two-year period in which the project manager prepares to implement the project culminating in a project agreement. The manager must prepare a series of deliverables during this time, including:
  - **Land management plan**
  - **Project management and governance plan**
  - **Monitoring and evaluation plan**
  - **Stakeholder engagement plan**
  - **Site access plan**
  - **Business model**
  - **Legal and contractual terms**
- **Project implementation,** wherein the project is executed according to the agreement.

The exact requirements for each phase may vary from round to round depending on the round objectives set out by DEFRA. However, the commonalities between the two completed rounds suggest likely focus areas which are covered in detail below.

Phase One: Application

During this phase, the applicant will assemble and submit their initial proposal for review. Project proposals must meet certain minimum

[188] https://www.gov.uk/government/publications/apply-for-landscape-recovery-funding/applicant-guidance-for-landscape-recovery-round-two#project-development-phase

requirements and designed with regards to specific environmental objectives as set out by DEFRA.

Both Rounds[189]

- **Size:** 500-5,000 hectares of broadly connected land.
- **Location:** All land must be within England
- **Applicants:** Public bodies must apply in collaboration with other land managers
- **Duration:** Projects will likely last more than 20 years
- **Funding:** Blended public and private. Private funding must be secured to complement public funding.

Round One[190]

- **Environmental objectives:**
    - **Recovering and restoring England's threatened native species**
        - Habitat quality
        - Habitat recovery
        - Species abundance

[189] https://www.gov.uk/government/publications/apply-for-landscape-recovery-funding/applicant-guidance-for-landscape-recovery-round-two#eligible-land

[190] https://www.gov.uk/government/publications/landscape-recovery-more-information-on-how-the-scheme-will-work/landscape-recovery-more-information-on-how-the-scheme-will-work#eligibility

- **Restoring England's streams and rivers**
    - Improving water quality
    - Improving biodiversity
    - Adapting to climate change

- **Scoring criteria:**
    - Environmental objective suitability
    - Project Longevity
    - Carbon and climate resilience
    - Social impact (public access, community engagement etc)
    - Project leadership and delivery
    - Costs

<u>Round Two</u>[191]

- **Environmental objectives:**
    - **Primary**
        - **Improving biodiversity**

[191] https://www.gov.uk/government/publications/apply-for-landscape-recovery-funding/criteria-and-scoring-guidance-for-landscape-recovery-round-two

      - Maintenance or restoration of protected sites or features, particularly sites of Special Scientific Interest (SSSIs)
      - Creation, restoration or effective management of wildlife-rich habitats outside of protected sites
    - **Net Zero**
      - Peatland restoration and maintenance
      - Woodland/tree planting, restoration or sustainable management
      - Sequestering habitat creation, maintenance or restoration, including
        - Salt marsh
        - Intertidal seagrass
        - Intertidal mudflats
        - Hedgerows
      - Carbon sequestering practices, e.g. regenerative agriculture
  - **Secondary**
    - Contribution to recovery of threatened species
    - Pollution reduction

- Support water-dependent biodiversity & flood prevention
- Reduce ammonia concentrations
- Reduce airborne particulate matter
- Use of landscape character
- Conservation of heritage assets
- Increase habitat resilience beyond primary objectives
- Reduce threat of invasive species
- Contribute to improved soil health
- Deliver other, unlisted environmental benefits

- **Scoring**
  - **Primary objective 1: Biodiversity** (25 points)
  - **Primary objective 2: Net Zero** (25 points)
  - **Secondary objectives** (20 points)
  - **Social impact** (10 points)
  - **Food production** (10 points)
  - **Value for money** (10 points)

Given the size and duration of qualifying projects, LR project applications require considerable paperwork. Specific application requirements will vary from round to round; the below were the requirements for round two applications.[192]

<u>Required application forms</u>

- Project proposal form
    - 100-word high level summary
    - 300 words on why the project qualifies for LR
    - 300 words on project manage responsibility and coordination
    - 300 words on main risks to the project's success
    - 300 words on how to mitigate aforementioned risks
    - 5,000 words on how the project will fulfil primary environmental objectives
    - 2,000 words on how the project will fulfil secondary environmental objectives
    - 1,000 words on project social impact
    - 1,000 words on project food production impact
- Land manager support form
- Project development costs form

---

192 https://www.gov.uk/government/publications/apply-for-landscape-recovery-funding/applicant-guidance-for-landscape-recovery-round-two#when-and-how-to-apply

Supporting evidence

- Maps
    - Project area land ownership and management
    - Current land use across project area
    - Proposed land use across project area
- Evidence of support from land managers (via land manager support forms)

Phase Two: Enrolment

Successful applications will then proceed to the enrolment phase. Background checks will be conducted by either Natural England or the Environment Agency to ensure project suitability. This includes ensuring that the project is represented by a **single legal entity**. Such an entity could be:

- The landowner or manager for projects on a single holding
- A lead land manager with authority to represent a group
- A single legal entity, e.g. a community interest company
- Another organisation authorized to act as an intermediary between parties

Following approval, the project will receive a development grant to fund the next phase.

Phase Three: Project Development

This is a two-year phase during which the project manager will produce a series of deliverables to lay the foundations for the project. Specific deadlines and deliverables will be set out in the initial grant funding letter. Deliverables will likely include:

- **Land management plan**, which describes what the project intends to achieve during implementation. This will include the project outcomes, activities carried out during implementation phase and long-term project considerations (e.g. how does the project factor in climate change over the 20-year implementation period?)

- **Project management and governance plan** which describes the project's governance and decision-making structure. This will also include key performance indicators, long-term legal safeguards and risk assessment and contingency plans.

- **Monitoring and evaluation plan** which describes how the project's environmental impact will be monitored and evaluated. This will include a baseline assessment of the current state of the land, the models used to predict outcomes, the frequency and methodology of monitoring and reporting, and a learning plan to share project outcomes and best practices.

- **Stakeholder engagement plan**, which identifies relevant stakeholders and how the project will engage with them, as well as the outcomes of engagement.

- **Site access plan**, which describes existing rights of way and how access infrastructure will be maintained and improved.

- **Business model**, which includes overall project costs, private investment sources and conditions, and risks to projected cashflow.

- **Finalization of legal and contractual terms**, including comprehensive legal agreements for funding from private sources and a final contract from the Landscape Recovery scheme.

During this period, Natural England or a relevant environment agency will be in regular contact with the project manager to monitor progress and provide guidance. The development phase will culminate in a project implementation agreement, which will set out the project outcomes and funding conditions.

Phase Four: Project Implementation

Once the project implementation agreement is signed, the project will be underway in earnest. Implementation agreements will include periodic reviews of payment rates and flexibility regarding project expansion. Implementation agreements are expected to be 20 years or longer, with review points every 3 to 5 years. DEFRA will reserve the right to end agreements that are not delivering agreed-upon outcomes.

CHAPTER SEVEN

LANDLORD & TENANT ISSUES

The Dasgupta Review on the Economics of Biodiversity[193] is further confirmation of our mismanagement of natural capital, because of a failure to value it correctly. Mistakes have been made both in terms of the process conducted by valuers and in the lack of appreciation of the important role it plays.

There is a need to have a standardised approach to auditing the stock of natural capital and to consider this alongside the conventional balance sheet. Only then can informed decisions be made about the sustainable use of our dwindling natural resources.

Landowners and tenants have many questions about their role in the stewardship and exploitation of natural capital and its associated value. Many of these questions have been prompted by the shift away from the Basic Payment Scheme, as set out in the Agriculture Act 2020 and the requirement in the Environment Act 2021 to increase biodiversity.

What is not in doubt, in the author's opinion at least, is that collaboration between landlords and tenants can lead to better environmental outcomes than the parties going it alone. The problem with the existing relationship of landlord and tenant is that it can very easily lead to a straitjacketed position of neither party being able to unlock the potential of the land to produce environmental services. The existing framework is focussed on agricultural productivity with the beneficial chaos of

---

[193] The Economics of Biodiversity: The Dasgupta Review (publishing.service.gov.uk)

scrubland habitat being regarded as part of a dilapidation claim and not the producer of biodiversity credits.

The dial is shifting with recognition from the government that tenants need more freedom to deliver both conventional agricultural and environmental outcomes. A useful way to illustrate the tensions that exist is to consider the fundamental issue of carbon and how an improved ability to sequestrate it might be treated in the context of the landlord and tenant relationship.

For such a market to operate efficiently, it will be necessary to establish:

- how much additional carbon has been sequestered by any specific measures taken;
- who owns the sequestration potential and the underlying carbon;
- legal mechanisms to quantify, define and transfer ownership of such potential; and
- confirmation that the sequestration potential can operate within existing carbon credit systems.

It must be stressed that this chapter is considering the ownership of the sequestration potential and not the valuation of any associated credits or tradeable instruments. This is about the ownership of the opportunity to lock up more carbon and any financial benefits that flow from that will be a function of the market place, which is evolving all the time.

<u>Opportunities</u>

In an agricultural context the prime movers for carbon sequestration are plants and the soil they grow in. The scale of UK farming and forestry means that it has a potentially huge role to play in taking CO2 out of the atmosphere and locking it up. It therefore makes sense to consider the control and use of these natural assets in assessing who can benefit from the process of increasing carbon sequestration.

However, a distinction has to be drawn between the ability to increase carbon sequestration and the existing bank of carbon stored in the soil and associated vegetation. It is the potential for increasing sequestration, which attracts the value, because that is the basis of the carbon credit market. If an airline is pumping CO2 into the atmosphere, it has to take an equivalent amount out and so maintaining the status quo will not be sufficient.

Obviously, ownership or ability to control the store and/or the potential may be different and that becomes very relevant in the context of the landlord and tenant relationship.

Freehold ownership

In order to analyse the landlord and tenant relationship, the extent of the fee simple absolute ownership needs to be considered. The fee simple absolute estate includes the soil, vegetation growing within it and the minerals lying in strata underneath it.

This is as comprehensive as real property ownership gets and if one considers that a freehold owner is entitled to remove mineral deposits, peat and even the top soil itself from his land, then that provides strong evidence that carbon stored within these components of ownership is also owned by the freeholder.

But are such rights included within the definition of mines and minerals, as the freeholder might have severed such rights and conveyed them away to a third party? *In Coleman v Ibstock Brick Limited [2008] EWCA Civ 73* the Court of Appeal considered the meaning of "minerals" in the context of a lease and found that it meant substances "exceptional in use, in value and in character" and did not mean the ordinary soil of the district.

That definition and the fact that carbon is in vegetation, root systems and topsoil in the main, points towards these rights not falling within the meaning of "minerals." The location of the carbon in the topsoil and upper layers is also not consistent with the definition of mines and minerals, which are inevitably in stratas of sub-soil beneath.

It follows that if the freeholder occupies the land then they will also control the sequestration potential of the land, through their management and husbandry of it. However, different considerations come into play if third parties are permitted to occupy.

As the market develops we may well need legislation to clarify the legal nature of ownership of sequestration potential, or to resolve how they are dealt with in a leasehold context.

The landlord and tenant relationship

If a leasehold interest has been granted then the terms of the lease will be important in clarifying what, if any, ability the tenant has to influence or control carbon sequestration, without obtaining the landlord's consent. Principally the relevant governing legislation here is the Agricultural Holdings Act 1986 (**1986 Act**) and the Agricultural Tenancies Act 1995 (**1995 Act**).

User clause

Most tenancy agreements will restrict the use of the holding to agricultural purposes only and so any carbon sequestration will have to be achieved within the definition of agricultural operations. That may be possible if the activities are based around soil improvement, such as increasing organic matter or varying crop rotations, subject to any permanent pasture restrictions etc.

However, the planting of trees or permanent crops by tenants is usually forbidden so that particular avenue of carbon storage will often be unavailable.

Further, the tenant will often be under a positive obligation to comply with the Rules of Good Husbandry (ROGH) which (along with the corresponding Rules of Good Estate Management) are the last surviving remnant of the Agriculture Act 1947. The problem for tenants, as with the definition of agriculture under any piece of legislation you care to consult, is that the ROGH are aimed at maximising production of agricultural commodities and not the provision of environmental benefits.

This focus on production means that activities like the creation of wild bird habitats, which utilise extensive conservation grazing, will not be possible because of the requirement in the ROGH to keep "permanent pasture properly mown or grazed and maintained in a good state of cultivation and fertility and in good condition" and "properly stocked."

However, carbon sequestration through husbandry, such as reduced or no tillage farming is squarely within the control and purview of the tenant, along with increasing soil biomass through increasing organic matter.

Entering agreements

The challenge for the tenant is then finding a scheme or commercial arrangement, which monetises the carbon sequestration. For tenancies under the 1986 Act an immediate potential problem arises from the term of the tenancy; tenants are invariably granted an annual periodic lease and therefore may struggle to enter into any credible long-term agreements with third parties.

The standard alienation provisions of an agricultural lease are unlikely to prevent a tenant from entering into a scheme, as acts of carbon sequestration are unlikely to involve sharing possession or occupation of the holding, never mind any sub-letting or assignment. Some alienation clauses, however, cast their net wider to prevent contract farming arrangements and these might possibly also catch a carbon offsetting agreement, but each lease will need to be individually reviewed.

However, tenants will not be able to enter into long term agreements which restrict how the land can be managed if a long fixed-term is required. For example, biodiversity net gain agreements with their 30-year minimum commitment for tenants will not be an option, but perhaps a market will emerge for short term commitments. Parties may also be willing to be more flexible given the security of a 1986 Act lease or in circumstances in which an FBT has several years left to run.

It must be stressed that the focus of this chapter is on private payments for environmental services and not public money in the form of financial assistance under the Agriculture Act 2020. Measures have already been taken in the 2020 Act to ensure that 1986 Act tenants are not excluded from claiming such annual payments by providing for the reference to arbitration of a landlord's refusal to consent or vary the terms of the tenancy.[194] The landlord and the tenant can instead agree to a third-party determination if they so wish.

The tenant's request must be either for a variation of the tenancy or a request for consent to enable the tenant to request or apply for financial assistance or to comply with a statutory duty. Financial assistance means that provided under section 1 of the 2020 Act which sets out a very broad range of purposes spanning environmental protection, heritage, access and agricultural production. The 2020 Act also gives power to allow the regulations to specify other conditions that have to be met by the tenant.

The purpose is to loosen the restrictions on tenants, which currently exist in tenancy agreements, so they have a better chance of being able to access funds in the new world of "public money for public goods". It is also with an eye to varying terms which prevent tenants undertaking activities to meet regulatory requirements, specifically environmental obligations. This is a clear move away from freedom of contract and gives third party oversight to the private landlord and tenant relationship.

194 Section 19A of the Agricultural Holdings Act 1986

It is notable that despite pressure from some quarters the right to refer such matters to arbitration or third-party determination was not also granted to 1995 Act tenants. DEFRA have indicated that this might change if they see evidence of landlords acting in a manner which necessitates such legislation.

The Welsh Government has ensured that both 1986 Act and 1995 Act tenants are provided with a dispute resolution mechanism, which will afford them the opportunity to override the terms of their tenancy agreements in certain circumstances.

Often tenancy agreements contain tenants' covenants preventing them from entering into subsidy schemes and from carrying out certain activities, that will likely be required as part of entry into such scheme (for example creating new woodland). Tenants require landlords' consent to enter into these schemes.

The Agriculture (Wales) Act 2023 (**AWA 2023**)[195] amends section 19A of the AHA 1986 to apply to Wales's financial support scheme. Wales are leading the way in affording ATA 1995 tenants the same opportunity. A new clause 8A is to be inserted into the ATA 1995. Tenants are permitted to refer disputes concerning requests for consent or variation of the terms of a tenancy to arbitration. Secondary legislation will bring into force Chapter 4 of the AWA 2023 in due course.

It will be interesting to see if there is a change in the tide in England given that DEFRA has already warned that it will legislate to allow ATA 1995 tenants to override these restrictions if landlords continue to control access to subsidy schemes.

Any landowners in England and Wales, who are currently negotiating new long term FBTs, should be aware that the Welsh provisions could come into force at any time and England could follow suit and pass new legislation, which could render any prohibition on the ability to enter

195 Chapter 4 (Section 24) AWA 2023

into any subsidy schemes ineffective. Collaboration between the parties is going to be key.

The Agriculture Act 2020 has laid the statutory foundation for moving financial support away from the EU focus on direct support to embrace environmental protection policies, designed to fulfil DEFRA's 25-year plan to improve the environment. However, the legislation governing landlord and tenant relationships in the agriculture sector and the customary contractual arrangements made under this legislation, sit uncomfortably with newly defined assets, such as natural capital and activities like the sequestration of carbon. The conservation covenants and biodiversity gain provisions included in the Environment Act 2021 may solve some of these issues in due course. That said, greater flexibility and imagination is going to be needed if tenancy legislation is going to fit more closely and the wider industry is to be weaned off a course of dealing between landlords and tenants, which has evolved with production as its primary focus. The world still needs to be fed but the landscape is different now and sustenance must be sustainable.

Recovering vacant possession

As the market for environmental service payments rapidly expands some landlords have seen a potential opportunity to recover possession of land from tenancies protected by the 1986 Act.

Many landlords are considering the opportunities that biodiversity net gain ("BNG") and nutrient neutrality represent, to say nothing of the existing carbon markets. All of these markets involve changes to the use and appearance of land whether that is habitat creation, cessation of farming or the management of woodland. The planting of trees from small copses to large scale afforestation can form part of these plans.

Definition of agriculture

It is therefore worth considering how the 1986 Act deals with the issue of tree planting. The question of purpose is the first consideration as the definition of agriculture states:

""agriculture" includes horticulture, fruit growing, seed growing, dairy farming and livestock breeding and keeping, the use of land as grazing land, meadow land, osier land, market gardens and nursery grounds, and the use of land for woodlands where that use is ancillary to the farming of land for other agricultural purposes, and "agricultural" shall be construed accordingly."

So where new woodland planting is planned for a use which is not ancillary to agricultural use that will result in a change of use of the land. It is suggested that the definition of agriculture was designed to deal with the planting of shelterbelts etc which are ancillary to the primary agricultural use of the land.

Agricultural or non-agricultural use?

The planting of trees for habitat creation purposes would, in the author's view, be a non-agricultural use and indeed in a nutrient neutrality context would have to be in order to demonstrate the required cessation of agricultural activity. It is possible that agricultural use could continue on lightly afforested land used for habitat creation, perhaps through extensive conservation grazing. In those circumstances there is arguably no change of use and the agricultural label remains firmly affixed. Whether or not a change of use has occurred is important because of the operation of the 1986 Act.

Planning permission

Although the planting of trees can effect a major change in the landscape, such an operation does not, of itself, require planning permission, although an Environmental Impact Assessment may be required from the Forestry Commission. This is despite the fact that there would be a change of use from agriculture to woodland.

Section 55 Town and Country Planning Act 1990 (**TCPA90**) defines "development" and development requires planning permission. It also identifies what is not development, and includes the following:

"(2) The following operations or uses of land shall not be taken for the purposes of this Act to involve development of the land—

[...]

(e) the use of any land for the purposes of agriculture or forestry (including afforestation) and the use for any of those purposes of any building occupied together with land so used"

The TCPA90 does not include a definition of "forestry" or "afforestation", but the Forestry Commission guidance on "Environmental Impact Assessments for woodland" (dated 28 September 2021) ("the Guidance") states:

"Afforestation means conversion of a non-woodland land use, for example agriculture, into woodland or forest (these terms are used interchangeably) by means of planting, or facilitating natural regeneration (self-sowing) of trees to form woodland cover. This can include proposals for short rotation coppice (SRC) and short rotation forestry (SRF), including energy crops and Christmas tree plantations."

Case B of the 1986 Act

If planning consent is not required, then a landlord will not be able to rely on the provisions of Case B of Schedule 3 of the 1986 Act. It must be remembered that there may be other aspects of a particular project which effect a change of use of the land or require development which may require planning permission.

Where perhaps Case B will come into consideration is where developers re-organise their projects to try and put landlords in a more favourable tactical position. If we consider the example of a redline development area of say 10 acres. Plans may be in existence to cover this with houses but the advent of the Environment Act 2021 ("EA 2021") and the need for BNG necessitates a change. Now the developer may require a redline area of 20 acres to accommodate the original number of dwellings plus the land required for onsite BNG mitigation.

SUDS

A further point here is the recent decision by the Government to implement Schedule 3 of the Flood and Water Management Act 2010, which makes Sustainable Drainage Systems ("SUDS") compulsory for all new development. This places a further burden on developers, who will have to acquire bigger sites or build fewer or smaller houses.

This new 20 acre combined development and mitigation site could be the subject of a new planning application, which if granted could found a valid Case B notice to quit. That is a very different proposition to the original 10-acre application with an accompanying purchase of the necessary BNG credits or similar mitigation provided on a separate site some distance from the development.

It does not seem likely that the extension of the development site to accommodate SUDS or BNG mitigation would invalidate a Case B notice to quit. This is because the BNG mitigation or SUDS within a development redline boundary would clearly be of a non-agricultural nature and would require planning consent as part and parcel of the housing development.

Renegotiation

In light of these developments, we might expect to see renegotiation of existing option and promotion agreements between developers and landowners or tactical discussions prior to the service of a notice to quit. The author's advice has always been that those tasked with getting planning permission should link up with those in charge of securing vacant possession as early as possible. That advice is even more relevant in the current climate.

Natural capital and section 27

Coming back to natural capital schemes, if a change of use is being effected from agricultural to woodland use then section 27 (3) (f) of the 1986 Act comes into play. That states:

27 Tribunal's consent to operation of notice to quit.

(1) Subject to subsection (2) below, the Tribunal shall consent under section 26 above to the operation of a notice to quit an agricultural holding or part of an agricultural holding if, but only if, they are satisfied as to one or more of the matters mentioned in subsection (3) below, being a matter or matters specified by the landlord in his application for their consent.

(2) Even if they are satisfied as mentioned in subsection (1) above, the Tribunal shall withhold consent under section 26 above to the operation of the notice to quit if in all the circumstances it appears to them that a fair and reasonable landlord would not insist on possession.

(3) The matters referred to in subsection (1) above are—

(a) – (e)……

(f) that the landlord proposes to terminate the tenancy for the purpose of the land's being used for a use, other than for agriculture, not falling within Case B.

Availing themselves of section 27 (3) (f) a landlord could therefore serve a notice to quit in circumstances where tree planting is proposed. However, there is an important safety net for the tenant; the Tribunal will not give consent to the operation of the notice to quit if they consider that a fair and reasonable landlord would not insist on possession.

<u>Fair and reasonable landlord</u>

On the face of it, it could be argued that a desire to tackle climate change through afforestation is a laudable aim and that a fair and reasonable landlord would therefore insist on possession. However, it may not always be the case that the average Tribunal would see things through such a macro lens.

The test is meant to be that of the hypothetical landlord and so objective in nature, but the Tribunal is human and inevitably, subjective views will be brought to bear. Every Tribunal will be different and one person's view of what is reasonable and the importance or otherwise of climate change etc may radically differ from another's. This is particularly so when the tenant's possible loss of home and livelihood is weighed in the balance.

Scale & context

Much may depend on scale and whilst consent might be given for possession of part of a holding, the economic and personal impact of losing a whole tenancy may well tip the scales in the tenant's favour – even in the face of the global emergency of climate change.

Similarly, context will play a part and if a landlord has a well worked up landscape scale recovery plan on the stocks, with one dissenting tenant blocking progress for the wider river catchment community, then that might swing the decision back into the landlord's camp.

Every case will be different and although we are working in a rapidly changing environment some things remain the same; that fundamental weighing up of the benefit to the landlord, as compared to the detriment suffered by the tenant, will still have to be performed by the Tribunal. Context is everything and early and sound professional advice will be essential.

CHAPTER EIGHT

GREEN FINANCE

Introduction

As discussed in the corporate market chapter, many public and private institutions are widening their investment philosophy to include environmental considerations, giving rise to green financing. While the exact meaning of the term may differ from source to source, this book will employ the World Economic Forum's definition of green financing as "any structured financial activity…that has been created to ensure a better environmental outcome."[196]

As the "green" nomenclature designates an investment objective rather than methodology, it can be applied to any existing financial instrument from bank loans to equity investments. Owners and agents of such instruments often offer additional incentives to encourage participation. Several UK banks, for example, offer "green mortgages" for energy-efficient homes at a discount to traditional mortgages.[197] The London Stock Exchange offers a "Sustainable Bond Market" platform for projects with "clear environmental benefits."[198] Governments—including the UK—issue "sovereign green bonds" and allocate the proceeds to environmental projects.[199] The term has even spilled into monetary

---

[196] World Economic Forum, "What is green finance?" Nov 2020 https://www.weforum.org/agenda/2020/11/what-is-green-finance/

[197] https://www.natwest.com/mortgages/mortgage-comparison/green-mortgages.html

[198] https://www.londonstockexchange.com/raise-finance/debt/our-products/sustainable-bond-market

[199] HM Treasury, "UK Green Financing Allocation Report,"

policy, with the UK,[200] EU,[201] US[202] and Chinese[203] central banks issuing guidelines on how they intend to integrate green financing into their decision-making process.

This chapter focuses on the UK approach to green financing: the government's green finance strategy, regulatory action, private sector participation, examples of green financial products, and how the sector will likely change in the coming years.

UK Government Green Finance Strategy

The UK Government has published its first green finance strategy in 2019, and its updated second strategy in 2023. The strategy identifies a national growth opportunity by financing a global transition to a "net zero, resilient and nature positive economy."[204] The government aims to do so by delivering on five objectives:

- **UK financial services growth and competitiveness.** The government recognizes that the UK's leading role in combatting climate change will likely be through its financial services industry and committed to supporting the sector's role in financing the global transition to net zero.

- **Investing in the green economy.** The government estimates that approximately £50-60 billion in capital investment will be required each year through the 2020s and 2030s. Facilitating that

---

200 https://www.bankofengland.co.uk/news/2021/november/boe-publishes-its-approach-to-greening-the-corporate-bond-purchase-scheme

201 https://www.ecb.europa.eu/press/pr/date/2021/html/ecb.pr210708_1~f104919225.en.html

202 https://www.federalreserve.gov/econres/notes/feds-notes/climate-change-and-financial-stability-20210319.html

203 http://www.pbc.gov.cn/english/130721/3133045/index.html

204 https://www.gov.uk/government/publications/green-finance-strategy/mobilising-green-investment-2023-green-finance-strategy

investment can help grow the UK economy and facilitate "leveling up" opportunities across the country.

- **Financial stability**. The government recognizes that climate change and environmental degradation pose volatility risks to any long-term investment and believes a green finance framework must provide the financial sector with sufficient information to manage risk appropriately.

- **A holistic approach.** The government strategy will incorporate both nature financing, such as projects that promote biodiversity, and climate financing, which focuses more on combatting climate change, in its green finance policy framework.

- **Aligning objectives with global financial flows.** The government's strategy is meant to support the global transition to net zero, including working with high-growth emerging markets and developing economies.

Given the enormous scope of the project involved, the government is organizing its different green finance policies into what it calls a Net Zero-aligned Financial Centre Framework (Net Zero Framework, NZF). The NZF "sets out how the government's green and sustainable finance policies work towards bringing about the net zero transition in the real economy and provide government oversight to ensure the shifting of financial flows"[205] and is divided into three areas: transparency, tools and transmission channels.

- **Transparency**. These policies reflect the need to ensure information and data is accurate, trustworthy and transparent. Policies in this category include sustainability disclosure requirements, financial product labelling and supporting

[205] https://www.gov.uk/government/publications/green-finance-strategy/mobilising-green-investment-2023-green-finance-strategy#chapter-1-foundations--uk-approach-to-green-finance-1

initiatives that improve global data tracking. Increased transparency is also meant to combat misleading or unsubstantiated claims relating to sustainability requirements, more commonly known as "greenwashing." In 2021, HM Treasury published a policy paper in which it set out its ambitions to establish "new economy-wide Sustainability Disclosure Requirements" and how those requirements may be implemented across different sectors of the economy; [206] these guidelines will be covered in more detail under the "UK Regulatory Action" section of this chapter.

- **Tools for transformation.** These policies emphasize the need to provide the financial services sector with the tools necessary to assist with the net zero transition. This includes the launch of the Green Taxonomy Advisory Group, which is developing recommendations on green financing taxonomy to standardize the market and combat greenwashing.[207] The results of such initiatives will likely form the foundations for the provision of green benchmarks and indices against which financial instruments may be measured. Education is another necessity: according to a 2022 PwC UK survey of small- and medium-sized enterprises, only 8% of respondents believe their firm is "highly prepared for future requirements in green and sustainable finance."[208] Organizations such as the Green Finance Education Charter, signed by professional associations such as Chartered

[206] https://www.gov.uk/government/publications/greening-finance-a-road map-to-sustainable-investing

[207] https://www.gov.uk/government/news/new-independent-group-to-help-tackle-greenwashing

[208] Green Finance Education Charter, "State of the Nation: Building Green and Sustainable Finance Capacity and Capability in UK Financial Services," https://www.charteredbanker.com/asset/37858EC7%2DCB0 B%2D4668%2D9085A6A58BFE5E0D/

Banker and the Chartered Institute of Securities and Investment, seek to educate financial professionals on green financing.

- **Transmission channels.** This category of policies is meant to de-risk green investments, broaden pools of capital and enable investors to influence corporate practice. Policy tools such as the Green Gilt programme, Solvency UK and the UK Infrastructure Bank are meant to facilitate this objective.

Net Zero-aligned Financial Centre Framework

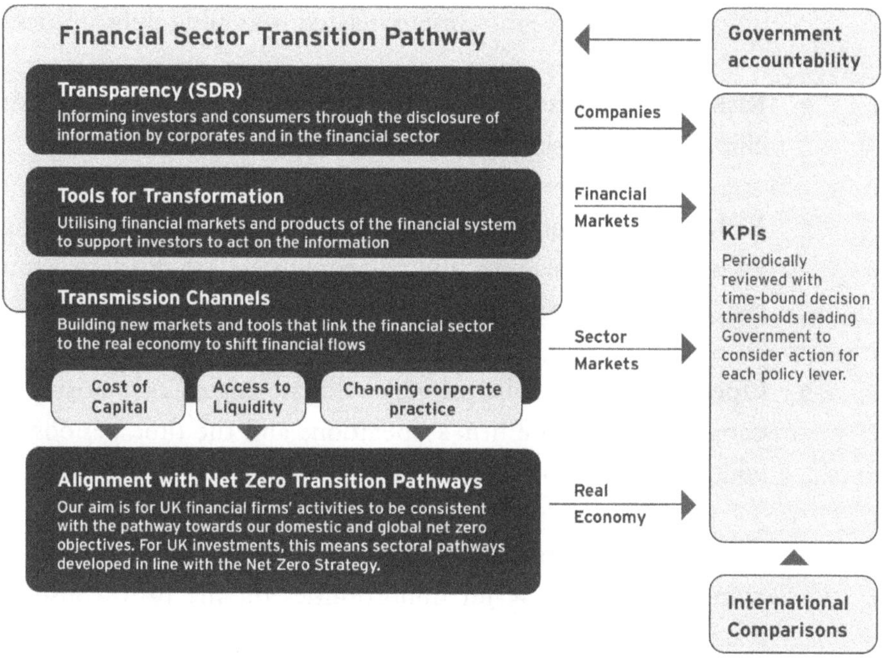

Source: Gov.uk 2023 Green Finance Strategy

UK Regulatory Action

Following government guidance, UK financial regulators have started implementing disclosure requirements for private companies, asset managers and financial products.

Corporates

In 2017, the Task Force on Climate-related Financial Disclosures set out 11 disclosure recommendations which broadly fall into four categories: governance, strategy, risk management, and metrics and targets.[209] In 2020, the UK Financial Conduct Authority (FCA) applied these disclosure requirements to premium listed commercial companies, then extended the disclosure requirement to standard listed equity shares the next year. Disclosure requirements include:

- **Governance:** The firm's governance arrangements in relation to assessing and managing climate-related risks and opportunities.

- **Risk management:** How the firm identifies, assesses and manages climate-related risks and opportunities.

- **Risk management integration:** How processes for identifying, assessing and managing climate-related risks are integrated into the firm's overall risk management process.

- **Operational risks:** The principal climate-related risks arising in connection with the firm's operations and the time periods by which such risks are assessed.

- **Climate change impact:** The actual and potential impacts of climate-related risks and opportunities on the firm's business model and strategy.

[209] https://www.fsb-tcfd.org/recommendations/

The guidance also highlights that "companies and LLPs should consider a range of transition risks and opportunities most relevant to their products and markets."[210]

Financial products

In November 2023, following several rounds of consultation the FCA published a policy statement on sustainability disclosure requirements and investment labels.[211] These requirements initially apply to UK asset managers overseeing UK fund products and portfolios. The regulator notes that tackling greenwashing is a "core regulatory priority," and that these regulations are meant to "help consumers…navigate an increasingly complex investment environment product landscape."[212] While the policy focuses on UK-based funds and portfolio managers, once established the FCA intends to review how they may be applied to overseas funds as well.

The proposals cover the following areas:

- **A general anti-greenwashing rule** which applies to all FCA-authorised firms and which will come into force on **31 May 2024**. The rule requires that "sustainability-related claims must be clear, fair and not misleading," with more specific rules for product names and marketing listed below.

- **Classification and labelling:** Products must qualify for a sustainability classification, which includes display of a label identifying the category for which the fund qualifies. To qualify, a financial product must evidence the following:

---

[210] https://assets.publishing.service.gov.uk/government/uploads/system/uploads/attachment_data/file/1056085/mandatory-climate-related-financial-disclosures-publicly-quoted-private-cos-llps.pdf

[211] https://www.fca.org.uk/publication/policy/ps23-16.pdf

[212] https://www.fca.org.uk/publication/consultation/cp22-20.pdf

- **Objective.** Have a clear sustainability objective that falls within one of the four below categories.

- **Investment strategy.** Invest at least 70% of the gross value of the product's assets in line with the relevant sustainability objective.

- **KPIs.** Firms must identify KPIs to measure progress against the stated objective.

- **Resources and governance.** The product must have appropriate resources allocated to support delivery of the stated objective.

- **Stewardship.** A stewardship strategy, including what activities will be taken to meet the objective/KPIs and an escalation plan if said activities do not demonstrate sufficient progress, must be identified and disclosed.

The product labels are:

- **Sustainability Focus:** product invests "in assets that are environmentally and/or socially sustainable, determined using the robust, evidence-based standard."

- **Sustainability Improvers:** product invests "in assets that have the potential to improve environmental and/or social sustainability over time."

- **Sustainability Impact:** product invests "to achieve a pre-defined positive, measurable impact in relation to an environmental and/or social outcome."

- **Sustainability Mixed Goals:** product invests in a mix of the above categories.

- **Disclosures:** The FCA notes that these proposals are "a starting point" and will be developed over time. The disclosure requirements fall into categories:

    - **Basic information:** Firm name, product name etc

    - **Product Label:** as set out in the "Classification and labelling" section.

    - **Sustainability goal:** the product's sustainability objective and impact on financial return, as well as progress made towards said objective.

    - **Sustainability approach:** a summary of how the product's strategy is meant to achieve the sustainability goal, e.g. investible universe. This section must include the types of assets held for reasons other than in pursuit of the objective and why (e.g. cash positions for liquidity and hedging)

    - **Sustainability metrics:** Any KPIs/metrics linked to achieving the objective or would help consumers better understand the approach taken by the financial product.

- **Naming and marketing rules:** These fall under the general "anti-greenwashing" rule to ensure all marketing is "clear, fair and not misleading, and consistent with the sustainability profile of the product or service." Sustainability-related terms such as "ESG," "climate," "responsible," "green," "Paris-aligned" or "net zero" may only be used if:

    - **They use the appropriate sustainability label, or**

    - **They comply with additional product name and marketing rules**, such as a prominently-placed statement clarifying that the product does not have a label and the reasons why.

- **Distribution rules:** This section regulates the intermediaries charged with distributing investment products to customers such as brokers and investment platforms. The proposed regulations require intermediaries to prominently display labels and provide access to consumer-facing disclosures, as well as disclaimers for overseas products that are not subject to FCA labelling. All labeling must be kept up-to-date.

Private Sector Participation

It is perhaps unsurprising given the prominence of green financing in the public arena that almost every market participant within the financial services industry offers some form of green financing as part of their business model. This section will provide an overview of how different participants are incorporating green financing into product suite.

- **Banks**. In addition to "green mortgages" discussed in the introduction of this chapter, banks also offer another suite of products that fall under the umbrella category of "green loans." These are typically loans made to individuals or small businesses for environmentally friendly purposes such as retrofitting buildings to enhance energy conservation or the acquisition of "green" assets such as electric vehicles or solar panels. These loans will typically be more advantageous than their standard equivalent. The NatWest green loan programme, for example, offers loans without arrangement fees or early repayment charges,[213] while Lloyds offers a 25-basis-point reduction on fixed-rate lending for green asset financing.[214]

213 https://www.natwest.com/business/loans-and-finance/sustainable-finance/green-loans.html

214 https://www.lloydsbank.com/business/commercial-banking/clean-growth-financing-initiative.html

- **Asset managers.** Out of 66,340 rated funds, ratings agency Morningstar lists 6,263 funds with a five-star sustainability rating.[215] These funds cover a wide range of locations and asset classes, from UK sustainable bond funds to Indian mid-cap equity funds.

- **Wealth managers.** Most wealth advisories now include sustainability objectives as part of their advisory services, with many family offices and high-end wealth managers like Coutts and UBS[216] advertising their sustainability credentials.

Tomorrow's Green Finance

The UK government will likely continue to come under pressure to support green financing. A February 2024 YouGov survey found that respondents believe environmental issues from pollution to habitat loss have worsened across the board over the past five years.[217] A March 2024 open letter to the Bank of England signed by over 60 economists and environmental activists[218] notes that progress in decarbonizing the Bank's balance sheet "appears to have stalled" and urged the BoE Governor to "re-prioritise work to align the financial sector with the government's climate goals."

On the retail side, banks and wealth managers alike will likely continue to burnish their green credentials given how prominent such concerns are for both the UK government and many UK consumers. Expect products such as green mortgages, green lending and sustainability-

215 https://www.morningstar.co.uk/uk/screener/esg

216 https://www.ubs.com/uk/en/wealth-management/our-services/sustainable-investing-solutions.html

217 https://d3nkl3psvxxpe9.cloudfront.net/documents/RoyalSociety_Environment_240228_w.pdf

218 https://positivemoney.org/wp-content/uploads/Letter-to-Andrew-Bailey-1.pdf

focused wealth managers to continue to feature within retail product suites.

On the institutional side, however, interest in green investment appears to have fallen. While quarterly inflows into ESG funds have plummeted from a high of US$184.1bn in 1Q21 to US$13.7 in 3Q23, flows have remained largely positive on the back of European investment. This has exposed a rift between EU asset managers who boast of their sustainability credentials, while their US counterparts have grown more taciturn on the subject.[219] In the UK, this downward pressure is likely to persist as the FCA cracks down on greenwashing and terms like "sustainability" become more heavily regulated. That said, passive sustainable financing—portfolios that rely on index tracking rather than active stock-picking—have grown substantially, more than doubling their market share over the past three years from 8.6% in 2020 to 20% in 2023.[220]

---

219 Brooke Masters and Patrick Temple-West, "The real impact of the ESG backlash," *Financial Times* 4 Dec 2023 https://www.ft.com/content/a76c7feb-7fa5-43d6-8e20-b4e4967991e7

220 https://www.ft.com/content/db819858-2600-41b1-b0bf-a1ada2aaba3d

CHAPTER NINE

TAXATION

Introduction

The rapid development of the natural capital asset market over the last few years has left the UK Government behind in ensuring that legislation and guidance on taxation matters is relevant and up to date. In the Spring 2024 Budget, the UK Government announced the creation of a working group consisting of representatives from HM Treasury and HM Revenue & Customs. This group will be tasked with clarifying the tax treatment of the production and sale of ecosystem service credits and associated units. DEFRA will also be asked to contribute.

The two areas where clarification has already been provided relates to inheritance tax (most specifically agricultural property relief (APR) and business property relief (BPR)) as well as value added tax. These will be set out in more detail below.

Amongst the flurry of the Spring 2024 Budget announcements, the Government published its long-awaited response to the consultation on the taxation of ecosystem service schemes.

This guidance appears to be a positive first step towards establishing a robust tax framework which will help facilitate the ongoing growth of the natural capital economy.

Agricultural Property Relief (APR)

In a move which will be much welcomed by landowners and advisers alike, the Government have confirmed that they will extend the existing scope of APR to include environmental land management from 6 April 2025. However, in the pre-election "wash up" period there was not time to pass any legislation confirming this extension and so we will have to wait and see what the next government decide to do.

The key points are:

- Relief will be available where the environmental land management scheme is entered into on or before 6 March 2024 (provided that it remains in place after 6 March 2024), but relief will only be available for lifetime transfers and transfers at death which take place **on or after 5 April 2025**.

- Relief will be available for land managed under an environmental agreement with or on behalf of the UK Government, Devolved Administrations, public bodies, local authorities or approved responsible bodies.

- Relief will continue to be available following the conclusion of an agreement, provided that it continues to be managed in a way which is consistent with the agreement.

- For the relief to apply, the land in question needs to have been agricultural land for **at least 2 years** prior to the change of land use, although interestingly one would not have to show that the land had been used for the purposes of agriculture or would have qualified for APR in its own right.

- Ownership period requirements for APR will not be restarted by land use change.

- The value of the relief will be based on a special assumption of a restriction as to its current use – presumably, much in the same way as "agricultural" values. Hope and development values will remain part of the open market value, which may have interesting implications for valuers and tax advisers if the open market value of the land extends beyond its "environmental" value (see further below).

- Farmhouses (and ancillary buildings) will qualify for relief if occupied with, and that occupation is ancillary to, environmental land.

The existing (and now long out of date) land habitat provisions set out in Section 124(c) of the Inheritance Tax Act 1984 will be repealed.

Business Property Relief (BPR)

- There are no proposed changes to the operation of BPR in this context, and the general rules will continue to apply. The availability of BPR will be assessed on a case-by-case basis in the usual way. BPR will continue to be available if the land in question forms part of a wider, composite, trading business (for example, in a "Balfour" context).

- The Government have also reaffirmed that the activities required to design, create, and maintain schemes falling within the Woodland Carbon Code and the Peatland Carbon Code are trading activities for BPR purposes.

- However, this guidance does not appear to go far enough to specifically confirm whether or not the activities required to develop and maintain other environmental schemes (including those involving Biodiversity Net Gain and Nutrient Neutrality, for example), would be deemed to be *trading* for BPR purposes.

- The activities carried out in each case will need to be carefully considered. However, in the absence of specific guidance, this may remain an area of uncertainty, and it will be interesting to see whether the draft legislation goes some way to redressing this in due course.

VAT

- The underpinning legislation for the VAT Terminal Markets Order (**TMO**) will be updated, including bringing trades in carbon credits within the scope of VAT and the TMO.

Working group with industry representatives

- The Government will be establishing a joint HM Treasury and HMRC working group tasked with clarifying the tax treatment of the production and sale of ecosystem service credits and associated units. DEFRA will also provide input.

Potential restrictions to APR

- The government have decided ***not*** to restrict APR to tenancies of at least 8 years. One of the deciding factors was that they felt it may lead to a contraction in the land available for tenant farmers. DEFRA will continue to work with the industry and look to support longer term tenancy agreements which retain flexibility.

- Environmental Land Management Schemes will also be accessible to tenant farmers, and this includes for tenants on shorter terms, on rolling annual tenancy agreements and on longer terms.

- Penalties will no longer be applied for tenants who have to exit a scheme early if their tenancy ends unexpectedly.

- Whilst tenants need to check the terms of their tenancy agreement before applying to SFI, SFI does not require the tenant to gain the landlord's consent although in the spirit of collaboration, the expectation is that the tenant would communicate with their landlord.

- DEFRA is also looking to ensure that more options are offered on shorter durations in their combined Environmental Land Management Scheme offer for 2024.

<u>Comment</u>

- The Government have clearly stated that the potential loss of APR should not be a barrier to land use change. This is a very welcome move and reassures landowners that they should not be forced to choose between (1) using their land in environmentally friendly ways for economic gain on the one hand and (2) the potential loss of valuable APR on the other. The guidance makes sense and seems to suggest that the legislation will follow the current APR framework closely, with ownership periods, farmhouses and ancillary buildings all covered. Draft legislation will be embodied in a future Finance Act, and we await sight of that with interest.

- That said, there is an argument to say that the change will not come soon enough – the relief will not be available on lifetime transfers or deaths until 5 April 2025.

- And the position in relation to BPR is less clear, with no proposed changes to incorporate environmental land usages. It had been hoped that the Government would offer further guidance in relation to whether activities required to run (for example) BNG and Nutrient Neutrality schemes could also be deemed to be trading (as they are for the Woodland Carbon Code and the Peatland Carbon Code).

- This "mismatch" with BPR could trigger some interesting valuation issues if the land used for environmental purposes is deemed to have a "hope" value above its agricultural / environmental value. The agricultural / environmental value would be covered by APR, but any "hope" value would not. This will provide further food for thought for landowners and advisers alike, particularly as valuations develop in this area.

- Overall, this is clearly very welcome news, particularly in relation to APR, which will provide some comfort for landowners as they continue to explore opportunities in this area.

- However, there remain a number of tax uncertainties (not least the treatment of payments received under ecosystem service schemes, and whether they income or capital), and so this feels like the first step along what will inevitably be a long road to an efficient framework for environmental taxation.

Direct Taxes, VAT and Inherence Tax: An Overview

The first part of this section is dedicated to the direct taxes which parties in the natural capital market may be exposed to. In the absence of any other guidance, this analysis falls back on the general principles of taxation and applies them in a hypothetical way. Part 2 deals in a limited way with Value Added Tax (VAT) and Part 3 consider inheritance tax (IHT) matters.

Part 1 – Direct Taxes

The Woodland Tax Exemption

The principle underpinning the woodland tax exemption (the **Woodland Exemption**) is that the commercial occupation of woodlands in the UK is not recognised as a trade for the purposes of Income Tax or Corporation Tax. This includes where the activities are undertaken with a view to realising profits. As the income derived from such operations is exempt, it follows that any expenditure incurred in the production of that income is not deductible. Losses arising from the carrying on of the commercial occupation of the woodland, are also not considered to be trading losses and may not be set off against other income.[221]

Capital allowances cannot be claimed on plant and machinery deployed for the woodland and no relief is available for expenditure incurred in the preliminary clearance of the woodland or other preparation of land used for the purposes of the commercial occupation of woodlands.[222] Note, the letting of land by a landowner to a third party for their commercial occupation of the woodlands is not covered by the exemption.

Whilst the Woodland Exemption is also extended to the chargeable gains tax regime by virtue of Section 250 of The Taxation on Chargeable Gains Act 1992, the exemption for *chargeable gains purposes* is specifically limited to the *sale of trees* from the woodland. This obviously has an impact if the capital value of woodland increases—and recently it has significantly done so.

The Woodland Exemption was, in the first instance, intended to apply to the growing and felling of trees i.e. forestry in its traditional sense. However, woodlands now play a much wider role in the development of multifunctional land and the maximisation of environmental benefits. Landowners are being encouraged to protect and enhance the natural environment and to see this activity as standing alongside their traditional roles of farming and food production.

As detailed in previous chapters, planting woodlands enables the sequestration of carbon, which in turn leads to the generation of carbon credits. These, along with any other monetised environmental benefits or services can be sold to the nature markets creating a new income stream for the landowner. Planting and managing biodiverse woodlands requires upfront investment in the establishment of the woodland and then ongoing management over a long period of time. Woodlands take time to reach the maturity required for carbon credits derived from those

---

221 Part 5, Chapter 8, Income Tax (Trading and Other Income) Act 2005.

222 BIM67701.

woodlands to carry value and enable their disposal to the nature markets. During that time there is economic activity to manage and sustain the woodland, although such activity might be offset by alternative environmental benefits or services. Initiatives such as the Woodland Carbon Code[223] actively encourage tree planting for the creation of woodlands.

The Woodland Exemption should apply to carbon related tree planting activities, although there is no confirmation that this is the case. There must be a strong argument for the extension of the Woodland Exemption to the activities of sequestering carbon in trees and creating and selling of carbon credits. Landowners are actively being encouraged to diversify the use of their land to help meet the Net Zero targets set by the UK Government. It is fully intended that landowners should participate in the nature markets which have developed around ecosystem services and be economically recompensed for that activity. This is commercial activity and planting or rehabilitation of woodlands is intended to achieve this commercial activity.

There is an obvious conflict between commercial forestry and the management of woodland for carbon sequestration purposes: the former is about growing trees in order to cut them down, and the latter has an assumption of permanence at its core. The Woodland Carbon Code will allow management of the woodland in order to maintain the average carbon sequestration claimed. That can include clear felling in part but the overall management plan must deliver the long term average carbon stock claimed for the scheme.

The government recognises the different uses of woodland and taxes them accordingly.

Woodland owners: tax guidance – GOV.UK (www.gov.uk)

---

[223] https://woodlandcarboncode.org.uk/about/the-basics

Environmental Benefits and Services Generally

Landowners who make their land available for other environmental services, for example biodiversity net gain or nutrient neutrality, will need to consider the following taxes and take professional advice in relation to their own circumstances.

Landowners who contract with third parties to provide environmental services on their land and receive a fee from that third party must understand how those payments are to be structured and what is to be given in return. The nature of the payment in the hands of the landowner will determine its tax treatment.

A payment received in advance and intended as an incentive to the landowner is likely to be of a capital nature in the hands of the Landowner. It would be taxable as a sum deriving from a capital asset (i.e. either the freehold or leasehold title owned by the landowner). Contrast that with a payment received by the landowner in return for services provided by the landowner. If this was a woodland, the Woodland Exemption should apply. However, for any other environmental service, this would be a taxable receipt in the nature of income. Again, this outcome is heavily dependent on the nature of the landowner, the terms of the agreement and the activities carried out.

Where recurring payments are received these are treated as being in the nature of income. They occur at regular intervals, are contractually fixed at the point of contract and usually last for the duration of the contractual arrangements. That said, in order for those payments to be subject to income tax, they must be received in the course of the carrying on of a trade. The courts and legislation have never developed a definitive, objective standard for the sort of activity which constitutes a trade. According to Section 989 of Income Tax Act 2007, a 'trade includes any venture in the nature of trade', while HMRC's guidance notes that 'trade' can be taken to refer to operations of a commercial kind by which the trader provides to customers for reward some kind of goods or services. The activity carried on by the landowner needs to have a commercial feel to it: it would be arms' length and be made in consideration of services provided and not the provision of land.

The exploitation of land for the provision of environmental services includes the production of various credits, which are broadly:

- Wood carbon
- Peat carbon
- Biodiversity Net Gain ("**BNG**")
- Nutrient Neutrality
- Credits which evidence environmental improvement used for corporate ESG Purposes ("**ESG Credits**"). These credits are the manifestation of the environmental improvement achieved and are underwritten by the habitat created or nutrient run-off mitigated.

Where it can be shown that the landowner is carrying out a trade in the provision of environmental services, the production and sale of carbon credits falls within the trading requirement such that income from these sales falls to be taxed as trading income. In the event there is insufficient activity by the landowner such that they cannot be said to be trading, the receipt of income from the sale of carbon credits is likely to be treated as investment income. As is discussed later, this has an impact on inheritance tax planning techniques.

Part 2 – Indirect Taxes

Up to this point, voluntary carbon credits have not been recognised as a credit under a statutory emissions regime such as the Kyoto Protocol or the EU Emissions Trading System (**EUETS**) 'cap and trade' regime. These credits are widely traded on national and international markets (HMRC regards them as compliance market credits) and standard rated for VAT accordingly.[224] By contrast, voluntary carbon credits are traded more privately and in HMRC's eyes their sale is outside the scope of VAT as there is no identifiable, direct benefit being received by the buyer in return for their money.

The UK government has now announced that with effect from 1 September 2024, the trade of voluntary carbon credits will attract value-added tax at the standard rate of 20%. In addition, the exemptions provided for in the VAT Terminal Markets Order (**TMO**) will be extended to voluntary carbon credits. Services falling within the exemptions will be zero-rated. The TMO contains the rules for determining the VAT liability of trades in commodities traded on specified markets. These developments mean that the VAT regime as it applies to carbon credits is becoming increasingly settled. Compliance market credits are already taxed at the standard rate. The announcement in relation to the voluntary carbon credits brings the two environmental credit regimes into alignment with each other.

Up to this point, voluntary carbon credits have not been recognised as a credit under a statutory emissions regime such as the Kyoto Protocol or the EU Emissions Trading System (**EUETS**) 'cap and trade' regime. These credits are widely traded on national and international markets (HMRC regards them as compliance market credits) and standard rated for VAT accordingly.[225] By contrast, voluntary carbon credits are traded more privately and until the amendments referred to above in HMRC's eyes their sale was outside the scope of VAT as there is no identifiable, direct benefit being received by the buyer in return for their money.

When considering whether VAT is chargeable on any environmental services provided by the landowner, the basic principle is that VAT is charged on the supply of a good or service made in return for

---

224 https://www.gov.uk/hmrc-internal-manuals/vat-supply-and-consideration/vatsc06584

225 https://www.gov.uk/hmrc-internal-manuals/vat-supply-and-consideration/vatsc06584

consideration. Whether or not the services provided by the landowner are sufficient to constitute a supply will depend on the nature of the services and the facts of the matter. The basic principle is that there must exist a business for VAT purposes. This can generally be distilled into a two-stage test, following the Court of Appeal decision in the recent case of *Wakefield College*:[226]

- Is the supply made for consideration? and

- Is the supply made for the purpose of obtaining income?

Part 3 – Inheritance tax (IHT)

Impact for Landowners

1 IHT primarily applies on the death of an individual, where the value of their estate, less any exemptions, allowances, and reliefs, is potentially subject to a 40% IHT charge. IHT can also be payable during an individual's lifetime, where assets are given away into trust or to a company.

2 In this section we consider the potential IHT implications for landowners contributing land to a natural capital scheme and entering into an appropriate agreement.

3 The contribution of land has the potential to affect the underlying IHT treatment of the land in the hands of a landowner. For the purposes of this chapter, we focus on two principal reliefs – Agricultural Property Relief and Business Property Relief – and comment briefly on Woodlands Relief and IHT conditional exemption.

---

[226] Wakefield College CoA – [2018] BVC 22.

Agricultural Property Relief (APR)

Background

4 APR can potentially apply (at 100% or 50% depending on certain circumstances) to relieve the agricultural[227] value of property / land occupied for the purposes of agriculture or environmental stewardship. For APR to apply:

4.1 the property / land must be used for the purposes of agriculture or environmental stewardship and owned by the transferor for a least 2 years (if they farm or steward it themselves) or 7 years (if it is farmed or stewarded by someone else);

4.2 the property / land must be agricultural[228] in nature; and/or

4.3 the land must be managed under an environmental agreement with or on behalf of the UK Government, Devolved Administrations, public bodies, local authorities or approved responsible bodies.

4.4 Relief will continue to be available following the conclusion of a stewardship agreement, provided that it continues to be managed in a way which is consistent with the agreement.

4.5 For the relief to apply, the land in question needs to have been agricultural land for at least 2 years prior to the change of land use, although interestingly one would not have to show that the land had been used for the purposes of agriculture or would have qualified for APR in its own right.

---

[227] The agricultural value is defined by section 115(3) IHTA 1984 as the value the agricultural property would have if it were subject to a perpetual covenant prohibiting its use other than as agricultural property.

[228] Section 115, IHTA 1984 provides a list of agricultural property.

Woodland

5 Woodland can qualify as agricultural property if it is occupied with, and that occupation is ancillary to, agricultural land or pasture,[229] for example woodland shelter belts, game converts or coppices grown for fencing materials. The purpose of the woodland must be to provide necessary support to the primary agricultural activities.

6 Woodland which is exploited commercially does not qualify as agricultural property for the purposes of APR but it can potentially qualify for BPR (please see further below).

7 It is generally accepted that where new woodland is planted as part of a woodland scheme for natural capital purposes, it would no longer be used for the purposes of agriculture for the duration of the natural capital scheme (and potentially beyond), but the new environmental stewardship aspect of APR would apply thereby relieving its agricultural value.[230]

8 Therefore, land contributed to a natural capital scheme by a landowner would no longer be used for the purposes of agriculture and so would only qualify for APR if it fulfils the criteria recently set out in the Spring Budget of 2024.

The Farmhouse

9 APR can apply to the agricultural value of a farmhouse if it is occupied with the agricultural land or pasture and is of 'character appropriate' to the agricultural property.

10 The availability of APR on a farmhouse is a complex area guided by caselaw. In simple terms, the farmhouse is the place from

[229] HMRC – IHT24032.

[230] HMRC confirm their interpretation in their guidance at IHTM25252.

which the farmer (the person who farms the land on a day-to-day basis)[231] conducts the farming operation.[232] In practice, the position is almost always more complex where (for example) farmers let land to others, enter partnerships and ultimately retire / cease to carry out agricultural activities.

11 When assessing whether a farmhouse is of 'character appropriate', HMRC base their approach on the *Antrobus*[233] case which sets out the main factors to be considered, including its size, layout, and content, whether it is 'proportionate' to the farming activities being carried out and how long the farmhouse has been associated with agricultural production. HMRC also apply the 'elephant' test – you know a farmhouse when you see one.[234]

12 Whilst each case would need to be considered on its own merits, the contribution of land to a natural capital scheme has the potential to alter the interpretation of whether a farmhouse is of 'character appropriate' to the wider farming operation. For example, if a landowner owns 300 acres of agricultural land which they farm in-hand, then a fairly large and grand farmhouse may be more likely to be of 'character appropriate' to the larger 300-acre farming operation than, say, 150 acres of land farmed in hand and another 150 acres contributed to a natural capital scheme, which does not qualify under the new APR ambit is no longer used for agricultural purposes.

13 Smaller farming businesses would potentially be more affected than, say, a larger farming enterprise where the land contributed to such a non-qualifying natural capital scheme comprises a smaller percentage of the whole. In each case, the landowner

[231] Lloyds TSB Banking v IRC [2005] (Antrobus II).

[232] CIR v John Whiteford and Son [1962] TR 157.

[233] Antrobus [2002] STC (SCD) 468.

[234] IHTM24051.

would need to take advice accordingly in respect of their own estate planning.

14 Contributing land to a natural capital scheme certainly has the potential to impact the 'character appropriate' test in respect of the farmhouse and the consequential availability of APR in each case. This could be a significant issue for some landowners depending on their individual circumstances.

15 Not all natural capital schemes will qualify for APR under the new rules. For example, catchment scale schemes entered into with water companies would not be eligible unless that entity also happened to be a responsible body. That is very unlikely to be the case where the agreement was entered into before the Spring Budget even though such schemes would otherwise qualify because of the retrospective nature of the new reliefs.

Business Property Relief (BPR)

Background

16 BPR is another potentially valuable relief from IHT which can apply on death or where qualifying assets are given away during lifetime. It can apply at 100% or 50% depending on the nature of the asset and who owns it.

17 To qualify for BPR, property must fall into categories of 'relevant business property' as set out by Section 105 Inheritance Tax Act 1984. Relevant business property includes a business (for example, a business carried out by a sole trader), an interest in a business (for example, a partnership share), shares in a trading company and land or buildings used in a business.

18 Section 105(3) IHTA84 states that a business carried on with the primary purpose of making or holding investments would not qualify as relevant business property for the purposes of BPR.

19 Accordingly, when assessing the nature of a business and the potential availability of BPR, the question becomes whether the business is 'wholly or mainly' trading (which would potentially qualify for BPR) or whether its business is wholly or mainly making or holding investments (which would not qualify for BPR). This is potentially very relevant in this context.

20 At SVM111150, HMRC set out their interpretation of the 'wholly or mainly' test, based on the judgement in *Farmer v IRC (1999) SpC 216*. The *Farmer* case involved a mixed-use estate comprising of both an in-hand farming business (accepted to be a trading activity) and let residential properties (deemed to be an investment activity – in other words, the collection of rents generated from an investment asset).

21 The *Farmer* case sets out that the following factors should be considered when assessing whether a business is wholly or mainly trading:

21.1 the capital (value) employed on the trading and investment sides of the business;

21.2 how much of the overall turnover is attributable to the trading and investment elements;

21.3 the profits resulting from the trading and investment assets;

21.4 the time spent by the landowner (and employees) on each of the trading and investment elements of the business; and

21.5 the overall context of the business when looked at 'in the round'.

22 These factors are not exhaustive or conclusive and, again, the interpretation of this area is governed by extensive caselaw.[235]

---

[235] HMRC v A.M. Brander (as executor of the Will of the late 4th Earl of Balfour) [2010] UKUT 300 (TCC).

However, the key point is that HMRC generally accept that an interest in a single, composite, wholly or mainly trading business *can* qualify for BPR, despite the assets of the business including what would ordinarily be deemed to be 'investment'[236] assets if considered on an individual basis.

Woodland Carbon Code

23 In this context, it is necessary to consider the specific tax treatment of land entered into schemes which are designed, validated, and verified in accordance with the Woodland Carbon Code (**WCC**).

24 In March 2023, HMRC released specific guidance relating to the WCC through IHTM25252, stating that:

"Land entered into and verified by these schemes to generate credits which can be sold to individuals, businesses or companies to off-set their emissions, or used to off-set the emissions of the landowner's business, will in principle qualify for business relief in their own right.

HMRC are of the view that the activities required to create manage and maintain the land for the purpose of generating credits will mean that any business undertaking these operations will, in general, be regarding as "trading" as opposed to holding or making investments, as required by Section 105(3) IHT84.

Where the business in question is generating credits under these Codes alongside other activities (i.e., farming) then the generation of credits and the land employed for this purpose will generally be considered a non-investment activity.

The units generated by the land in question, including "pending issuance units" (PIUs) – effectively a promise to deliver a carbon credit

[236] Excluded as relevant business property under Section 105(3) IHTA84.

in future, based on predicted sequestration – will also qualify for BPR providing they are used in, or are an asset of, a qualifying business".

25 The position for a landowner carrying out these activities themselves, at their own risk and expense, is therefore clear cut – the activities required to create, manage, and maintain the land for the purpose of generating credits is a deemed to be a 'trading' activity for the purposes of BPR. As a natural consequence, the land contributed to a WCC project by a landowner stands to qualify for BPR in their own right, as would the PIUs.

26 However, the position becomes much less certain where WCC projects are established alongside a third-party SPV under contract with the landowner, as is envisaged here.

BPR eligibility of the Natural Capital Scheme – Landowner's perspective

27 The investment exception set out at Section 105(3) IHTA84 is again very relevant to this analysis. It is envisaged that the Landowner will contribute land to a natural capital scheme and run it under a contractual arrangement with an SPV. Accordingly, the question becomes whether the landowner is deemed to be carrying out the trading activities listed in IHTM25252 (to design, create and maintain the natural capital scheme) so that BPR potentially applies, or whether, because of the involvement of the SPV, they are deemed to be owning and holding land as an investment in order to generate income (and other payments), which would preclude the availability of BPR.

28 One can exploit land and property for profit in a variety of ways – on one side of the spectrum, a landowner can simply grant a tenancy and receive rents (an investment activity) and on the other the landowner could be providing an exceptional level of

service by running a hotel or shop from a premises (a trading activity).[237]

29 The question here is where the natural capital scheme should fall within that spectrum, and whether the activities carried out by the landowner are deemed to be trading or investment, given the involvement of the SPV.

30 The caselaw again provides guidance in this area:

30.1 In *McCall v Revenue and Customs Commissioners [2009] NICA 12*, a landowner entered into grazing agreements which allowed the grazier to exploit the land for payment. The land was not used to provide any service distinct from the use of the land, and the landowner simply collected rents, despite remaining in possession of the land (i.e., no formal lease or tenancy was granted). The landowner was denied BPR despite arguing that they were in the business of providing a service – the landowner's activities were limited to essentially receiving rents and they did not provide additional services. Therefore, the investment exception applied.

30.2 In *Furness v Inland Revenue Commissioners [1999] SPC 202*, the business consisted of investment income (the rental of caravans) and trading income (from caravan sales and the provision of additional services such as a bar and a shop). Overall, the business was deemed to be trading as opposed to investment on the basis that the provision of extra (trading) services outweighed the investment element.

30.3 In Pawson *(Deceased) v Revenue and Customs Commissioners [2013] UKUT 050 (TCC)*, it was held that a business which consisted solely of service holiday lets would be very unlikely to qualify as relevant business property unless an 'exceptional' level

237 Inland Revenue Commissioners v George [2003] EWCA Civ 1763.

of service was provided by the landowner – in that context, a 'hotel' level of service.

31 Therefore, it is sensible to assume that HMRC would require the landowner to provide a high (or even exceptional) level of service as part of its obligations under any agreement. They may argue that there would need to be a degree of commerciality required akin, say, to a Share Farming Agreement, where each party contracts with the other on a fully commercial basis and there is no 'value shifting' from one party to another.

Woodlands Relief

32 Woodlands Relief can apply where neither APR nor BPR apply. It is a relief which applies on death to relieve the value of the timber growing on the land (but not the value of the underlying land itself). In practice, the relief only stands to defer the IHT charge on the value of the timber – when the timber is sold or given away, IHT would be payable on its market value as at the date of disposal.

33 When considering whether or not to elect for this relief to apply, the executors of the landowner's estate would need to consider the underlying value of the timber (which is likely to be of far less value than the underlying land) and whether a deferral of IHT on that value would be prudent, given that the timber is unlikely to be sold during the duration of the Agreement).

34 Whilst very much a last resort in the absence of APR and BPR, Woodlands Relief is potentially worth considering by the executors of a landowners' estate on death.

IHT Conditional Exemption

35 Woodland which is of outstanding scenic, historic, or scientific interest can qualify for conditional exemption from IHT if certain conditions are met. As part of the conditional relief,

HMRC would usually impose strict conditions the landowner in respect of maintenance and public access.

36 On the basis that any the woodland created by a natural capital scheme would be highly unlikely to qualify under this exemption, we do not consider it further here.

Structuring efficiencies for Landowners

37 As set out above, there may be some natural capital schemes which don't qualify for the new APR. Accordingly, before entering into the Landowner Agreement, the landowner may wish to consider potential estate and tax planning strategies of their own to mitigate their potential IHT liability.

Lifetime Planning

38 In the expectation that APR and BPR may not apply to the land once it is contributed to the natural capital scheme, the Landowner could consider transferring the land to their heirs *before* they enter the natural capital scheme, so that the IHT risk essentially passes down a generation.

39 If the transfer is made with no strings attached (i.e., the landowner does not retain any benefit in the land given away) the value of the land will leave their estate for IHT purposes if they survive seven years from the date of the transfer. Accordingly, the landowner would have succeeded in transferring value down a generation, and the loss of APR / BPR would not be an IHT issue on their death. It could, of course, remain an issue in the hands of the next generation.

40 The obvious disadvantage to giving the land away is that the landowner would be deprived of the capital and income generated by the natural capital scheme. However, depending on cash flow requirements and in the context of overall retirement

and succession planning, it could be a helpful tool in ensuring that value cascades down a generation.

41 It might also be possible in certain circumstances for landowners to insure against the IHT risks through the use of life assurance policies. The attractiveness of this option would again depend on cash flow and the commercial and financial viability of protecting against the risk. If the BPR risk only applies for a limited period (i.e., if a claim for BPR is more likely to be accepted after year five), then it might be possible to insure against this specific risk for a limited time only.

Maintaining or establishing a composite, wholly or mainly trading business

42 The analysis above sets out how the Land contributed to a natural capital scheme could be caught by the investment exception at Section 105(3) IHTA84, so that it fails to qualify for BPR in its own right.

43 However, even if the land is deemed to be an investment for the purposes of Section 105(3), its value could still be relieved from IHT if it formed part of a wider, composite business which remained wholly or mainly trading for BPR purposes.

44 This follows the judgement in *HMRC v A.M. Brander (as executor of the Will of the late 4th Earl of Balfour) [2010] UKUT 300 (TCC)* which established that it was acceptable for an element of investment activity to form part of an overall trading business, provided that the business was still 'wholly or mainly' trading.

45 The tests set out at 21 above are very relevant here too. If a landowner's farming business consists of sufficient trading assets (in this context, land farmed in-hand with a view to generating profit), such that the business would still be wholly or mainly trading notwithstanding the existence of the natural capital scheme land held as an investment, then the interest in the overall

business (including the investment land) *can* still qualify for BPR, provided that all conditions are met.

CAPITAL GAINS TAX (CGT)

Impact on Landowners

46 CGT is charged on any growth in value of certain capital assets (over and above the value at which they were acquired) which are disposed of or deemed to be disposed of by individuals, personal representatives, or trustees.

Is participation in a natural capital scheme agreement a disposal for CGT purposes?

47 The key question to be considered is whether the entry into *a natural capital scheme* agreement by the landowner constitutes a disposal for CGT purposes.

48 Such an agreement is not a lease or a tenancy in a legal sense, and it is not designed to transfer an interest in land. Therefore, it is not a disposal or part disposal of an interest in land for the purposes of Section 21 (2)(b) TCGA 1992.

49 However, any upfront payment would be chargeable to CGT in the hands of the Landowner (or corporation tax for companies) as the receipt of a sum deriving from a capital asset under Section 22(1)(d) TCGA 1992.

50 There are interesting valuation issues which will essentially underpin the tax consequences in this area. Of key importance is the question of whether the natural capital scheme agreement affects the underlying capital value of the land in the hands of the landowner. One could argue that there are three possible outcomes:

50.1 The agreement *devalues* the Land in the hands of the landowner on the basis that the SPV gains rights over the Land which restrict its use (akin to a lease).

50.2 The agreement *increases* the capital value of the Land in the hands of the landowner because of the additional income stream generated (although we would expect a valuation based on an income stream basis to be lower than a valuation based purely on capital values).

50.3 The agreement does not impact the capital value of the land.

51 If the agreement causes non-commercial value to shift from one party to another then it could, on the face of it, be a taxable event. Given the existing structure of the agreement and the overall scheme, any potential tax consequences as a result of the value shifting would need to be carefully considered.

Ongoing CGT consequences for the Landowner

52 If the agreement generates a CGT event for the landowner, the landowner can explore various methods of mitigating their potential liability. Again, the extent to which this is necessary will depend on the values involved.

53 We highlight these briefly below and the availability or otherwise of these reliefs will depend on the nature and underlying structure of the landowner's farming business, and of the nature of the disposal. In each case, there would also be numerous conditions to be satisfied for the reliefs to apply and we should also say that the reliefs may not operate concurrently.

(i) **Business Asset Disposal Relief (BADR)**

53.1.1 Depending on the nature and underlying structure of the landowner's farming business, BADR could apply to apply a

CGT rate of 10% to qualifying gains up to a lifetime limit of £1 million.

(ii) Rollover relief on replacement of business assets

53.1.2 Where all conditions are satisfied, rollover relief under Sections 152-159 TCGA 1992 can be available if the landowner makes a disposal of certain business assets and uses those proceeds to acquire new business assets.

53.1.3 If the relief applies, the chargeable gain on the disposal is deferred until the landowner disposes of the new business assets.

(iii) Holdover relief

53.1.4 If assets used in a trade are disposed of at less than full market value, holdover relief under Section 165 TCGA 1992 may be available to be claimed by the landowner.

53.1.5 If the relief applies, the chargeable gain on the disposal is effectively deferred until the assets are subsequently disposed of by the transferee.

CHAPTER TEN

SCOTLAND, WALES AND NORTHERN IRELAND

Overview[238]

A cornerstone principle of UK constitutional law is parliamentary sovereignty: that the UK Parliament has the supreme legal authority to create legislation which will apply across England, Scotland, Wales and Northern Ireland. This is in contrast to federal systems like that of the United States, which balances legislative authority across local, state and federal levels.

While Westminster retains absolute authority, in recent years it has granted a greater level of legislative autonomy to Scotland, Wales and Northern Ireland through the passage of various acts in a process known as "devolution." As a result, the Scottish Parliament, Welsh Senedd and the Northern Irish Assembly are able to pass legislation on local matters that fall within their devolved competence. Furthermore, under what's known as the Sewel Convention, the UK Parliament will not normally legislate on devolved matters without having first sought the consent of these local institutions.

Environmental and agricultural policies are both devolved matters; as such, the majority of the regulation discussed in this book is applicable only to England. Scotland, Wales and Northern Ireland have separate regulatory frameworks which will be discussed in this chapter. It must

238 David Torrance, "Introduction to devolution in the United Kingdom," House of Commons Library 15 November 2023 (https://researchbriefings.files.parliament.uk/documents/CBP-8599/CBP-8599.pdf)

also be stressed that the devolved nations are, in some respects, somewhat behind England in progressing the market for environmental services. This statement is caveated because both Scotland and Wales have an abundance of natural resources which they have many years of experience in managing. What they lack is a clear legislative framework to govern the creation and operation of nature-based markets. At the time of writing Wales has enacted the Wales (Agriculture) Act 2023 but its own Environment Act 2016 is some 5 years older than the EA 2021 and the focus of that legislation is at much more of a macro level. Drilling down into farm scale schemes and solutions will require further legislation in due course.

Environmental Regulation

A significant aspect of English biodiversity net gain legislation is that it provides a quantitative framework for the new regime: developers must achieve a 10% net gain, as defined via a series of metrics. If they are able to provide a realistic plan for achieving this, they may have a reasonable expectation that, all else being equal, local authorities should grant the application. This also bolsters their case for appeal and judicial review should the local authority turn down their application without sufficient cause.

By contrast, Welsh, Scottish and Northern Irish biodiversity schemes do not provide a quantitative framework for biodiversity net gain. This gives local authorities greater discretion to consider applications on their individual circumstances and merits, but decreases developer certainty that their applications will be approved provided they meet certain pre-defined criteria.

Wales

Welsh planning authorities have a general duty to maintain and enhance biodiversity. The government does so via what it calls the "Net Benefits for Biodiversity" (NBB) policy. Biodiversity enhancement must be included as part of a planning application "unless other significant material considerations indicate otherwise."[239] Planning authorities should make reference to local context and ecosystem resilience attributes when assessing an application. The NBB policy does not include quantifiable metrics and provides planning authorities with greater discretion in determining whether an application maintains and enhances biodiversity.[240]

Legal Framework

- Well-being of Future Generations (Wales) Act 2015 (link)
- Environment (Wales) Act 2016 (link)

Both of these acts impose duties related to biodiversity on local authorities. Section 3 of the Well-being of Future Generations (Wales) Act 2015 imposes a duty on public bodies to carry out "sustainable development," and take into account "the importance of balancing short term needs with the need to safeguard the ability to meet long term needs, especially where things done to meet short term needs may have detrimental long term effect" (s 5(2)(a)). Section 6 of the Environment (Wales) Act 2016 imposes a general duty on public authorities to "seek to maintain and enhance biodiversity in the exercise of functions in relation to Wales" and take ecosystem diversity into account as part of this duty (s 6(2)(a)).

Where England's BNG framework provides a quantifiable method for demonstrating biodiversity, local authorities in Wales have wider discretion in interpreting how to discharge their section 6 duty. However, government guidance makes it clear that planning authorities "must seek

239 "Biodiversity enhancements: guidance for heads of planning." https://www.gov.wales/biodiversity-enhancements-guidance-heads-planning

240 https://www.britishecologicalsociety.org/caffi-ecology-net-benefits-for-biodiversity/

to maintain and enhance biodiversity in the exercise of their functions"[241] and that planning permission must be refused if environmental damage cannot be avoided or mitigated.[242] Furthermore, as biodiversity considerations are not confined by administrative boundaries, when drawing up their planning application applicants must also include consideration of the development's impact on adjoining planning authorities.[243]

Part of this duty includes taking ecosystem resilience into account based on five attributes specified in the Environment (Wales) Act: Diversity, Extent, Condition, Connectivity and Aspects of ecosystem resilience. The Chartered Institute of Ecology and Environmental Management summarises the five attributes as follows[244]:

- **Diversity**: maintaining and enhancing diversity at every scale, including genetic, structural, habitat and between-habitat levels. This supports the complexity of ecosystem functions and interactions that deliver services and benefits.

- **Extent**: incorporating measures which maintain and increase the area of semi-natural habitat/features and linkages between habitats. In general, smaller ecosystems have reduced capacity to adapt, recover or resist disturbance.

- **Condition**: The condition of an ecosystem is affected by multiple and complex pressures acting both as short term and longer term types of disturbance. Both direct and wider impacts should be considered, for example avoiding or mitigating pressures such as

---

241 Welsh Planning Policy 11th Ed para 6.4.5 (p. 137) https://www.gov.wales/sites/default/files/publications/2021-02/planning-policy-wales-edition-11_0.pdf

242 Welsh Planning Policy 11th Ed para 6.4.4 (p. 137)

243 Ibid.

244 https://cieem.net/wp-content/uploads/2022/08/Net-Benefits-briefing.pdf

climate change, pollution, invasive species, land management neglect etc.

- **Connectivity**: This refers to the links between and within habitats, which may take the form of physical corridors, stepping stones in the landscape, or patches of the same or related vegetation types that together create a network that enables the flow or movement of genes, species and natural resources. Developments should take opportunities to develop functional habitat and ecological networks within and between ecosystems, building on existing connectivity.

- **Aspects** of ecosystem resilience (adaptability, recovery and resistance): ecosystem resilience is a product of the above four attributes. Adaptability, recovery and resistance to/from a disturbance are defining features of ecosystem resilience.

Welsh Government's Approach to Net Benefits for Biodiversity and the DECCA Framework in the Terrestrial Planning System, CIEEM Briefing Paper September 2022

In addition to the most up-to-date ecological information available, government guidance provides three authorities to which planning authorities must have regard when discharging their section 6 duty:[245]

- the list of habitats and species of principal importance for Wales, published under Section 7 of the Environment (Wales) Act 2016

- the State of Natural Resources Report from Natural Resources Wales[246]

245 Welsh Planning Policy 11th Ed para 6.4.6 (p.137)

246 https://naturalresources.wales/evidence-and-data/research-and-reports/state-of-natural-resources-report-sonarr-for-wales-2020/?lang=en

- any Area Statement covering the area (in whole or in part) in question.

What this means for developers

Developers will need to include a biodiversity component to their planning application. There is no standardized list of requirements that will satisfy a planning authority; instead, developers will need to include a bespoke report detailing the site's biodiversity and ecological resistance, as well as what steps the developer will take to minimize impact on the site and increase biodiversity. Natural Resources Wales has provided guidance and examples on introducing sustainable management[247] and ecosystem resilience.[248]

Scotland

The Scottish government initially opted to handle biodiversity via policy rather than legislation, having drafted a National Planning Policy to tackle climate change and nature recovery.[249] Scottish nature falls under the purview of NatureScot, Scotland's nature agency.[250] Like Wales, the Scottish approach is qualitative rather than quantitative, relying on the professional judgement of ecologists rather than specific metrics. In September 2023, the government published a research paper considering a more quantitative approach for site-level biodiversity measurements.[251] The paper recommended a "common framework" be developed through

247 https://cdn.cyfoethnaturiol.cymru/media/693356/resilient-ecological-networks-practitioner-guide.pdf

248 https://naturalresources.wales/guidance-and-advice/environmental-topics/land-management/ecosystem-resilience-field-guide/?lang=en

249 https://www.gov.scot/publications/scotland-2045-fourth-national-planning-framework-draft/pages/5/

250 https://www.nature.scot/about-naturescot

251 https://www.gov.scot/publications/research-approaches-measuring-biodiversity-scotland/pages/2/

a bundle of metrics. However, such a framework has not been implemented at time of writing.

Relevant legislation

- Nature Conservation (Scotland) Act 2004 (https://www.legislation.gov.uk/asp/2004/6/contents)

Section 1 of the Nature Conservation (Scotland) Act 2004 imposes a duty on every public body and officeholder to "further the conservation of biodiversity" in the exercise of their functions and have regard to any biodiversity conservation strategy designated by the Scottish government (s 2(1)). In December 2022, the Scottish Government published its draft "Biodiversity Strategy to 2045"[252] . The strategy sets a goal of restoring and regenerating Scottish biodiversity by 2045 by implementing a series of Priority Actions, including introduction of statutory targets via a Nature Environment Bill, development of a Biodiversity Investment Plan and establishment of a "values-led, high-integrity market for responsible private investment in natural capital."[253]

In September 2023, the Scottish Government sought commentary on elements of the proposed Nature Environment bill.[254] The consultation includes the proposed actions:

- **Overall:** Drive cross sectoral action by introducing a framework for statutory nature restoration targets in the proposed Natural Environment Bill

[252] https://www.gov.scot/publications/scottish-biodiversity-strategy-2045-tackling-nature-emergency-scotland/

[253] https://www.gov.scot/publications/scottish-biodiversity-strategy-2045-tackling-nature-emergency-scotland/pages/2/

[254] https://www.gov.scot/publications/tackling-nature-emergency-consultation-scotlands-strategic-framework-biodiversity/

- **Woodlands:** Identify and facilitate partnership projects for six large scale landscape restoration areas with significant woodland components by 2025 and establish management structures with restoration work progressing by 2030.

- **Woodlands:** Support landowners to protect and restore priority ancient woodlands by 2030, where the initial priority list is those protected/designated woodlands that are currently in unfavourable condition.

- **Peatlands:** Develop a national peatland monitoring framework that incorporates on-site and remotely sensed assessments of biodiversity indicators, climate resilience and associated functions within the wider landscape, hydrological and ecological network contexts.

- **Marine:** Develop a new approach to marine biodiversity monitoring, including testing through pilots, covering both state and pressure work.

30 by 30

In April 2024, the Government published a consultation paper seeking views on legislative proposals for Scotland to meet a commitment to protect 30% of its land and seas by 2030. This policy, which the government dubs "30 by 30," is a "key delivery mechanism"[255] for implementing the biodiversity strategy set out in December 2022.

The first section involves introducing greater flexibility towards management of protected areas. The government defines protected areas as "SSSI (Sites of Specific Scientific Interest), European Sites (Special Protection Areas (SPA) and Special Areas of Conservation (SAC)) and

[255] https://www.gov.scot/publications/meeting-30-30-commitment-terrestrial-freshwater-sites-consultation-legislative-proposals/pages/2/

Ramsar sites."[256] The report notes that the "static nature of the designation" means "there is little or no flexibility to adapt management to changing circumstances" such as changes to a habitat in response to fluctuating flora/fauna population levels. Reforms are meant to allow for a "holistic management of ecosystems."[257]

The second section notes that, as a lack of positive management of a site is "unlikely to be classed as damage under current provisions," NatureScot therefore relies primarily on voluntary management agreements with landowners. Some enforcement mechanisms exist: for SSSIs, NatureScot can seek Land Management Orders (LMO) and Nature Conservation Orders (NCO) under the Nature Conservation (Scotland) Act should the land owner/occupier refuse to enter into a management agreement. Such orders are effectively compulsory management agreements. However, these orders are limited in scope and are meant to be used as a last resort. The report therefore proposes explore implementing a wider range of interventions by amending existing provisions for LMOs and NCOs and possibly expanding their scope to cover a wider range of categories.

The paper also proposes that a mechanism be developed to identify areas where there are significant gains to be made in meeting biodiversity and climate objectives via implementation of specific management actions. Doing so would give NatureScot greater flexibility in setting a regulatory framework, as well as providing access to financial support and advice.

Northern Ireland

Section 1 of the Wildlife and Natural Environment Act (Northern Ireland) 2011 places a duty on every public body "in exercising any functions, to further the conservation of biodiversity so far as is consistent

256 https://www.gov.scot/publications/meeting-30-30-commitment-terrestrial-freshwater-sites-consultation-legislative-proposals/pages/2/

257 https://www.gov.scot/publications/meeting-30-30-commitment-terrestrial-freshwater-sites-consultation-legislative-proposals/pages/3/

with the proper exercise of those functions."[258] In 2016, the Northern Ireland Department of Agriculture, Environment and Rural Affairs published guidance to public bodies in executing this duty.[259] It identified five aspects of biodiversity that needs to be taken into account:

- **Protecting biodiversity** by taking into account existing biodiversity as part of an initial appraisal of new projects or programmes

- **Maintaining biodiversity** by ensuring mechanisms are in place on lands owned or managed by the public body

- **Enhancing biodiversity where possible** by seeking opportunities to do so

- **Restoring biodiversity** on sites within the public body's ownership or influence

- **Raising awareness of biodiversity** both inside and outside the organisation

A December 2023 report by the Chartered Institute of Ecology and Environmental Management (CIEEM) notes that "there is no formal legislation or policy regarding Biodiversity Enhancement in the Republic of Ireland or Northern Ireland."[260]

258 https://www.legislation.gov.uk/nia/2011/15/crossheading/biodiversity

259 https://www.daera-ni.gov.uk/publications/biodiversity-duty

260 https://cieem.net/wp-content/uploads/2023/12/CIEEM-Breifing-Paper-on-Biodiversity-Enhancement-in-Ireland.pdf

Agricultural Regulation

Wales

Welsh agricultural policy is in a major state of transition, with the first Senedd-produced agricultural Act having received royal assent in August 2023. The Agriculture (Wales) Act 2023 is a wide-ranging act covering topics ranging from setting out a framework for agricultural support based on sustainable land management objectives to providing a route to dispute resolution for tenant farmers.

Section 1 of the Act establishes four objectives towards sustainable land management (SLM):

1. Provide food and other goods in a sustainable manner (s 1(2))

2. Mitigate and adapt to climate change (s 1(3))

3. Maintain and enhance ecosystem resilience (s 1(4))

4. Conserve, enhance and promote public access to the countryside and cultural resources (s1(5))

Welsh ministries now have a duty to exercise certain functions in a manner that contributes to achieving the SLM objectives, as well as powers to provide support for agricultural (and ancillary) activities such as promoting animal welfare standards and improving air quality. Ministries must also prepare an annual report detailing the financial and non-financial support they provide and an Impact Report every five years on the effectiveness of said support.

Section 21 of the Act also empowers ministers with the power to intervene in agricultural markets in the event of what they consider to be "exceptional market conditions." These powers include the ability to provide financial support to agricultural producers whose incomes are adversely affected by the exceptional market conditions.

Forestry

Sections 34 to 41 of the Act amend the Forestry Act 1967, elevating the National Resources Body of Wales (NRW) as the Welsh forestry authority. The Act empowers the NRW to impose conditions on or revoke tree felling licences in order to preserve natural beauty or natural habitats.

Wildlife

Sections 43 to 45 make it an offense to set certain kinds of traps to catch wildlife, such as snares or glue traps.

Scotland

The Scottish government introduced the Agriculture and Rural Communities (Scotland) bill to the Scottish Parliament in September 2023.[261] As of writing, the Bill has passed the first debate and is at the amendments stage of the process. If passed as introduced, the Bill will give Scottish Ministers the power to establish an agricultural framework which will be brought into law via secondary legislation. It sets out the following agricultural policy objectives:

1. The adoption of sustainable and regenerative agricultural practices,

2. The production of high-quality food

3. The facilitation of on-farm nature restoration, climate mitigation and adaptation

4. The enabling of rural communities to thrive.

[261] https://bprcdn.parliament.scot/published/2023/11/24/39b120ec-5b30-4af2-8633-3665d5902cbf/SB%2023-44.pdf

Like the Welsh Act, the Scottish Bill will empower ministries to provide support to agricultural producers "in such a way that Scottish Ministers consider appropriate" and intervene in agricultural markets during exceptional market conditions. Ministers may also delegate responsibilities to agencies such as NatureScot.

MORE BOOKS BY LAW BRIEF PUBLISHING

A selection of our other titles available now:-

'A Practical Guide to the Independent School Standards – September 2023 Edition' by Sarah McKimm
'A Practical Guide to Estate Administration and Crypto Assets' by Richard Marshall
'A Practical Guide to Managing GDPR Data Subject Access Requests – Second Edition' by Patrick O'Kane
'A Practical Guide to Parental Alienation in Private and Public Law Children Cases' by Sam King QC & Frankie Shama
'Contested Heritage – Removing Art from Land and Historic Buildings' by Richard Harwood QC, Catherine Dobson, David Sawtell
'The Limits of Separate Legal Personality: When Those Running a Company Can Be Held Personally Liable for Losses Caused to Third Parties Outside of the Company' by Dr Mike Wilkinson
'A Practical Guide to Transgender Law' by Robin Moira White & Nicola Newbegin
'A Practical Guide to 'Stranded Spouses' in Family Law' by Mani Singh Basi
'A Practical Guide to Residential Freehold Conveyancing' by Lorraine Richardson
'A Practical Guide to Pensions on Divorce for Lawyers' by Bryan Scant
'A Practical Guide to Challenging Sham Marriage Allegations in Immigration Law' by Priya Solanki
'A Practical Guide to Digital Communications Evidence in Criminal Law' by Sam Willis
'A Practical Guide to Legal Rights in Scotland' by Sarah-Jane Macdonald
'A Practical Guide to New Build Conveyancing' by Paul Sams & Rebecca East
'A Practical Guide to Defending Barristers in Disciplinary Cases' by Marc Beaumont
'A Practical Guide to Inherited Wealth on Divorce' by Hayley Trim
'A Practical Guide to Practice Direction 12J and Domestic Abuse in Private Law Children Proceedings' by Rebecca Cross & Malvika Jaganmohan

'A Practical Guide to Confiscation and Restraint' by Narita Bahra QC, John Carl Townsend, David Winch
'A Practical Guide to the Law of Forests in Scotland' by Philip Buchan
'A Practical Guide to Health and Medical Cases in Immigration Law' by Rebecca Chapman & Miranda Butler
'A Practical Guide to Bad Character Evidence for Criminal Practitioners by Aparna Rao
'A Practical Guide to Extradition Law post-Brexit' by Myles Grandison et al
'A Practical Guide to Hoarding and Mental Health for Housing Lawyers' by Rachel Coyle
'A Practical Guide to Psychiatric Claims in Personal Injury – 2nd Edition' by Liam Ryan
'Stephens on Contractual Indemnities' by Richard Stephens
'A Practical Guide to the EU Succession Regulation' by Richard Frimston
'A Practical Guide to Solicitor and Client Costs – 2nd Edition' by Robin Dunne
'Constructive Dismissal – Practice Pointers and Principles' by Benjimin Burgher
'A Practical Guide to Religion and Belief Discrimination Claims in the Workplace' by Kashif Ali
'A Practical Guide to the Law of Medical Treatment Decisions' by Ben Troke
'Fundamental Dishonesty and QOCS in Personal Injury Proceedings: Law and Practice' by Jake Rowley
'A Practical Guide to the Law in Relation to School Exclusions' by Charlotte Hadfield & Alice de Coverley
'A Practical Guide to Divorce for the Silver Separators' by Karin Walker
'The Right to be Forgotten – The Law and Practical Issues' by Melissa Stock
'A Practical Guide to Planning Law and Rights of Way in National Parks, the Broads and AONBs' by James Maurici QC, James Neill et al
'A Practical Guide to Election Law' by Tom Tabori
'A Practical Guide to the Law in Relation to Surrogacy' by Andrew Powell
'A Practical Guide to Claims Arising from Fatal Accidents – 2nd Edition' by James Patience
'A Practical Guide to the Ownership of Employee Inventions – From Entitlement to Compensation' by James Tumbridge & Ashley Roughton
'A Practical Guide to Asbestos Claims' by Jonathan Owen & Gareth McAloon

'A Practical Guide to Stamp Duty Land Tax in England and Northern Ireland' by Suzanne O'Hara
'A Practical Guide to the Law of Farming Partnerships' by Philip Whitcomb
'Covid-19, Homeworking and the Law – The Essential Guide to Employment and GDPR Issues' by Forbes Solicitors
'Covid-19 and Criminal Law – The Essential Guide' by Ramya Nagesh
'Covid-19 and Family Law in England and Wales – The Essential Guide' by Safda Mahmood
'A Practical Guide to the Law of Unlawful Eviction and Harassment – 2nd Edition' by Stephanie Lovegrove
'Covid-19, Brexit and the Law of Commercial Leases – The Essential Guide' by Mark Shelton
'A Practical Guide to Costs in Personal Injury Claims – 2nd Edition' by Matthew Hoe
'A Practical Guide to the General Data Protection Regulation (GDPR) – 2nd Edition' by Keith Markham
'Ellis on Credit Hire – Sixth Edition' by Aidan Ellis & Tim Kevan
'A Practical Guide to Working with Litigants in Person and McKenzie Friends in Family Cases' by Stuart Barlow
'Protecting Unregistered Brands: A Practical Guide to the Law of Passing Off' by Lorna Brazell
'A Practical Guide to Secondary Liability and Joint Enterprise Post-Jogee' by Joanne Cecil & James Mehigan
'A Practical Guide to the Pre-Action RTA Claims Protocol for Personal Injury Lawyers' by Antonia Ford
'A Practical Guide to Neighbour Disputes and the Law' by Alexander Walsh
'A Practical Guide to Forfeiture of Leases' by Mark Shelton
'A Practical Guide to Coercive Control for Legal Practitioners and Victims' by Rachel Horman
'A Practical Guide to the Law of Driverless Cars – Second Edition' by Alex Glassbrook, Emma Northey & Scarlett Milligan
'A Practical Guide to TOLATA Claims' by Greg Williams
'A Practical Guide to Elderly Law – 2nd Edition' by Justin Patten
'A Practical Guide to Responding to Housing Disrepair and Unfitness Claims' by Iain Wightwick

'A Practical Guide to the Law of Bullying and Harassment in the Workplace' by Philip Hyland
'How to Be a Freelance Solicitor: A Practical Guide to the SRA-Regulated Freelance Solicitor Model' by Paul Bennett
'A Practical Guide to Prison Injury Claims' by Malcolm Johnson
'A Practical Guide to the Small Claims Track – 2nd Edition' by Dominic Bright
'A Practical Guide to Advising Clients at the Police Station' by Colin Stephen McKeown-Beaumont
'A Practical Guide to Antisocial Behaviour Injunctions' by Iain Wightwick
'Practical Mediation: A Guide for Mediators, Advocates, Advisers, Lawyers, and Students in Civil, Commercial, Business, Property, Workplace, and Employment Cases' by Jonathan Dingle with John Sephton
'The Mini-Pupillage Workbook' by David Boyle
'A Practical Guide to Crofting Law' by Brian Inkster
'A Practical Guide to the Law of Domain Names and Cybersquatting' by Andrew Clemson
'A Practical Guide to the Law of Gender Pay Gap Reporting' by Harini Iyengar
'NHS Whistleblowing and the Law' by Joseph England
'Employment Law and the Gig Economy' by Nigel Mackay & Annie Powell
'A Practical Guide to Noise Induced Hearing Loss (NIHL) Claims' by Andrew Mckie, Ian Skeate, Gareth McAloon
'An Introduction to Beauty Negligence Claims – A Practical Guide for the Personal Injury Practitioner' by Greg Almond
'Intercompany Agreements for Transfer Pricing Compliance' by Paul Sutton
'Zen and the Art of Mediation' by Martin Plowman
'A Practical Guide to the SRA Principles, Individual and Law Firm Codes of Conduct 2019 – What Every Law Firm Needs to Know' by Paul Bennett
'A Practical Guide to Adoption for Family Lawyers' by Graham Pegg
'A Practical Guide to Industrial Disease Claims' by Andrew Mckie & Ian Skeate
'A Practical Guide to Conducting a Sheriff Court Proof' by Andrew Stevenson
'A Practical Guide to Vicarious Liability' by Mariel Irvine
'A Practical Guide to Applications for Landlord's Consent and Variation of Leases' by Mark Shelton
'A Practical Guide to Relief from Sanctions Post-Mitchell and Denton' by Peter Causton

'A Practical Guide to Equity Release for Advisors' by Paul Sams
'A Practical Guide to Financial Services Claims' by Chris Hegarty
'The Law of Houses in Multiple Occupation: A Practical Guide to HMO Proceedings' by Julian Hunt
'Occupiers, Highways and Defective Premises Claims: A Practical Guide Post-Jackson – 2nd Edition' by Andrew Mckie
'A Practical Guide to Financial Ombudsman Service Claims' by Adam Temple & Robert Scrivenor
'A Practical Guide to Running Housing Disrepair and Cavity Wall Claims: 2nd Edition' by Andrew Mckie & Ian Skeate
'A Practical Guide to Holiday Sickness Claims – 2nd Edition' by Andrew Mckie & Ian Skeate
'Arguments and Tactics for Personal Injury and Clinical Negligence Claims' by Dorian Williams
'A Practical Guide to Drone Law' by Rufus Ballaster, Andrew Firman, Eleanor Clot
'A Practical Guide to Compliance for Personal Injury Firms Working With Claims Management Companies' by Paul Bennett
'RTA Allegations of Fraud in a Post-Jackson Era: The Handbook – 2nd Edition' by Andrew Mckie
'RTA Personal Injury Claims: A Practical Guide Post-Jackson' by Andrew Mckie
'On Experts: CPR35 for Lawyers and Experts' by David Boyle
'An Introduction to Personal Injury Law' by David Boyle

Milton Keynes UK
Ingram Content Group UK Ltd.
UKHW021115110724
445464UK00003BA/6